To Virginia, 6-2-00

Heaven Help Me!
A Celestial Guide To Healing

Blessings to you, Nancy Freier & Shebela

Nancy Freier
Foreword by Timothy Wyllie

Also by Rev. Nancy Freier

YOU CAN TALK TO YOUR ANGELS – A workbook and a two-part guided meditation tape to help you connect with your angels and guides in spirit. This is the same method Rev. Nancy Freier teaches in her workshops. For information about the workshops, workshop schedule and to host a workshop, visit the website at:
http://theinnervoice.com/workshop.htm

PRAYERS AND MEDITATIONS FROM THE ANGELS – An audio tape you can listen to at any time and feel the presence of the angels and hear their enlightening words. Read by the author, some of the prayers are from this book.

THE INNER VOICE MAGAZINE
http://theinnervoice.com – Published in print from 1991-1998, it has been online since 1997. Visit monthly for magazine updates featuring various authors and health practitioners. Take part in the Spiritual First-Aid message exchange board and a world-wide prayer ministry.

Please visit the Lightlines Publishing website at:
http://theinnervoice.com/lightlines.htm

Heaven Help Me!

A Celestial Guide To Healing

Nancy Freier
and Sreper, Angel of the Great White Light

Lightlines Publishing Company
Palm Desert, California

Copyright ©1999 by Nancy Freier

Published in the United States by
Lightlines Publishing Company
P.O. Box 2838,
Palm Desert, CA 92261-2838
(760) 568-9802
E-mail: lightlines@theinnervoice.com
Website: http://theinnervoice.com/lightlines

Edited by Diane Kaminski

Cover art "Aurora" ©1997 Fred Casselman.
Courtesy Earth Echo Project, an oasis of peace, love and divine light on the web
at http://www.earthecho.com

The author of this book does not dispense medical advice or prescribe the use
of any such technique as a form of treatment for physical or medical problems
without the advice of a physician, either directly or indirectly. The intent of the
author is only to offer information of a general nature to help you in your quest
for emotional and spiritual well-being. In the event you use any of the information in this book for yourself, which is your constitutional right, the author and
the publisher assume no responsibility for your actions.

Library of Congress Cataloging-In-Publication Data
Freier, Nancy
Heaven Help Me! A Celestial Guide For Healing/Nancy Freier and Sreper,
Angel of the Great White Light.
ISBN 1-930126-02-6 (trade paper)
1. Spirit writings. 2. Mind-Body 3. Angels-Miscellanea. I Title.
BF1343.F862   1999   99-068081
133.93 –dc21   CIP

ISBN 1-930126-02-6
10 9 8 7 6 5 4 3 2 1
First Printing, December 1999

Printed in the United States of America

Acknowledgements

First of all, I thank God for the ability I have been given to hear the angels talk to me. It has saved my life! Their beautiful messages inspired me and countless others to wake up and see life differently, to make necessary changes and to see miracles. The people who helped bring this unique communication about were, first of all... Rita Tarkinow, Bob Watzke and the late Al Welch.

I would like to acknowledge Joann Baumann for her unwavering miracle-mindedness. Since we met in 1986, she has never failed to be there for me and she has continually encouraged my work to unfold. Thanks for your on going love and support, and for all those late night talks!

I would like to thank all the people who asked the angels for help, for they are the pioneers in trusting this information. They tested it, their lives changed and their suffering suddenly had meaning. Perhaps some of these people weren't aware how deeply moving this information really was – of course, I had a unique vantage point. I read every message that came through, and the information was stunning. Patterns emerged. What the angels said to one person needed to be told to many. I learned something from every one of your questions and I thank you. I learned how universal we all really are. May the questions that were asked of the angels somehow alleviate the agony others may be experiencing.

A great source of inspiration that has changed my life from the inside out is a book called *A Course In Miracles*. Several passages from it are included in this book. I also thank those who studied it with me for I learned miracles can and do happen.

A piece of my heart goes to Jerome Surdyk whose death

awakened me and to my late friend, Al Welch who taught me a great deal about life after death. And now you are there and I hope that it is everything you said it was and more. May you both be smiling at me now.

I thank my mom for her love and support; my dad for his quiet strength; my older brother, Steve Freier for being born first to show me the way, and for his loving 'brotherly advice' throughout the years – if I wanted it or not, including how to escape from the playpen when I was little. You have always been there for me and perhaps now I can return the favor and bring the healing gift of the angels to you. *I know you can heal yourself!* Call on your angels, then listen with your heart... they are there for you! My younger brother, Michael, for his influence of eating a healthy diet and for his delicious sense of humor.

My deepest gratitude goes to Jim Clark for believing in me and seeing that this book was published. Jim's love and guidance all the way through this project made this book a reality. Thank you, Jim. I love you, honey!

I want to acknowledge authors Louise Hay and Meredith Young-Sowers whose books enlightened and inspired me greatly. You lit a fire! You have both touched my heart in a very deep place. I hope to follow in your footprints and carry that torch to many others.

There are my personal friends and earth plane travelers who have encouraged or influenced me in some way: Rita Tarkinow for teaching me automatic handwriting; Beverly Kay for predicting I would become a writer and publisher long before I knew it; Jonnie Dvorak for her friendship; Christopher Pearce for his astrological forecasts and his silliness; Richard Jerome Bennett who has got to be one of the most talented musicians on the planet; Bev Bâby for sharing so many heart-felt moments with me; Sue Franz for coming into my life twice; and Kathleen Jacoby whose keen insights about life light up the world.

You are my stars and I thank each and every one of you! You have blessed my life. And now may God likewise bless those who are touched by this book.

To my bj

Table of Contents

Foreword by Timothy Wyllie

Author of *Dolphins, ET's & Angels* and co-author
of the international bestseller *Ask Your Angels*

Heaven Help Me! A Celestial Guide To Healing will be a valuable tool for those reaching out for angelic guidance in these turbulent times. The Voice is strong, trustworthy, humorous, always compassionate, and carries the limitless encouragement of the angelic perspective. Meditating on, and truly taking to heart, the graceful counsel of Nancy Freier's celestial companion will open the reader to a reality that we have all but forgotten; that we are individually loved and cared for by the angels, by God, and by the Universe, to a degree that we might think quite impossible.

The angels are here with us to work together to help transform the planet, but first, there is the internal work to be done. *Heaven Help Me! A Celestial Guide To Healing* gently encourages us to face our demons, to send them back to the Light and to take on our true life's path with a fearlessness and an integrity that draws from an authentic angelic connection.

Working with our angels is a natural and righteous part of our evolution as spiritual beings in a physical world. This book, *Heaven Help Me! A Celestial Guide To Healing* amply illustrates the wisdom and the vision of just such a collaboration. I hope it will reach many.

♥

Miracles I've Seen

As A Result of Sreper's Guidance

by Joann Baumann, Holistic Healer

B eautiful messages of hope and comfort came to Nancy from an angel, Sreper and as a result, made profound changes in the lives of those to whom the messages were given, and to hundreds of others who have read them. Over many years in my healing practice, I asked Nancy for Sreper's guidance for my clients and for myself. As I applied the angel's love and wisdom in my work, I witnessed first hand dozens of miracles.

One of the most remarkable cases of Sreper's heavenly help was for a young boy who was diagnosed as being mentally retarded and autistic. At age four, he didn't speak. The information given by Sreper as to why the boy was having these conditions and what needed to be done were the keys that would open the door and bring about the healing. The angel's words freed him from his little world! This also involved some healing for other members of his family, as well. Changes began to occur immediately after the first healing session, and within six months, the boy came out of his shell and was talking normally. He started kindergarten in special education, and by first grade he was attending a mainstream school. Sreper's wisdom guided me all along to bring the miracles about.

When my 19 year-old son, Terry died accidentally in a fire, I sought Sreper's wisdom through Nancy to find out why his life had ended so abruptly and at such a young age. The angelic communication with my son's spirit lovingly showed me that we were still connected despite the death of his earthly body.

Sreper's message was extremely comforting to me and

had preceded a profound healing of my grief on the eve of his funeral. Though Sreper's beautiful predictions left some questions in my mind (a common thread in angel readings as their words always lead us into the future), a short time later, his prophecies of how Terry would work with me from 'the other side' began to come true. From Sreper's message I learned that there were no accidents and that Terry's 'return to Love' on that side was perfect in God's plan, as Sreper said. I was able to heal. Many people have since been inspired and healed by these beautiful and comforting words of this glorious angel.

Many of Sreper's messages were printed in *The Inner Voice* magazine between 1992 and 1998. These messages have been shared with inmates in my spiritual awareness classes in jails, and have been mailed to numerous other inmates in prisons elsewhere. Sreper's loving guidance has brought inspiration for healing, change and angelic experiences to those behind bars. The heavenly guidance in this book is timeless and extremely powerful. It is helpful to all who are seeking answers and relief for any earthly problem.

Joann Baumann is a miracle-minded spiritual healer and minister with a private practice in the State of Wisconsin. She uses acupressure, Reiki, iridology and nutrition in her work. She facilitates *A Course In Miracles* classes and produces a television program on healing and miracles in Milwaukee, Wisconsin. Joann writes a column called *Miracles I've Seen* for *The Inner Voice* magazine (online at http://theinnervoice.com). A part of her healing ministry takes her inside prisons and half-way houses where she helps deeply troubled individuals find love, health, faith and contentment. As a healer, Joann has seen many "incurable" illnesses reversed. Her work and commitment to helping others is inspiring and thanks to her support, this book was possible.

Preface

"A happy outcome to all things is sure."
-A Course In Miracles

Talking to angels isn't a new thing. There are many books on this subject today, but back in 1986 when my fiance´ died suddenly, there was an angel inside my head talking to me. His name is Sreper (pronounced "sir repper") and he describes himself as an *Angel of the Great White Light.* Trust me, there weren't many books or understanding people to turn to for help back then. Looking back at that time now, I see that it was my call to awaken, as though an alarm clock had been set to go off when I reached that point of complete despair in living my life my way, without angelic guidance. It was time to fling back the shutters and let the Light in. The angels were shouting from somewhere deep inside of me, and I knew it was time to listen.

On the other hand, I hadn't heard of anything so absurd! *What do you mean, talk to angels? Was I going nuts?* Well, maybe I was. I even went to sign myself into a psychiatric hospital about a month into having these internal conversations, convinced I must have made a wrong turn somewhere in my life to have this problem added to the mix of others equally debilitating that preceded it. Wasn't the death of my boyfriend enough? Did I have to lose my mind too?

But, if losing my mind led to the eventual healing of many men, women and children of some deep emotional hurts and life-threatening illnesses, then so be it, I am certifiable. But, if we pause for a moment and ask ourselves, "What do angels really do?" I guarantee you will hear an answer – *their answer* – the answers they have been waiting forever to tell us. And, if we could learn to trust this wisdom to guide us to the resolutions of our earthly problems, then listen up... this book is for you!

Let the words of the Creator, delivered on the wings of

angels, simplify the complexity of your mind, your illness, or your life. Let go and let God! And, we let God by allowing His Angelic Messengers to deliver His healing grace. I suggest you try it. I suggest we all try it.

Let this book be the beginning of a happy journey back to total health and happiness – as God would have us be. My wish is that you take the words in this book – the illuminating healing words of the Heavenly angels, and put them in your heart.

♥

A Call to Awaken

We've all had light bulbs go off in our heads just in time to get us out of a jam, to enlighten us, or to show us a different way to see a situation. I have learned that these flashes of light, these moments of spontaneous clarity, are the angels managing to intervene with their wisdom and love precisely at the moment it is needed.

Several years ago, following the sudden and tragic death of my fiancé, Jerry Surdyk, my guardian angel Sreper, Angel of the Great White Light, began talking to me. The volume was turned up and I began to listen. The messages were comforting. They served to heal my heart and eventually the angel's wisdom allowed me to let go of the devastating sorrow I felt, and to move on with my life. These healing messages that I had received over the years, plus my desire to provide information to others, inspired me to create and publish a magazine called, "The Inner Voice."

Readers told me Sreper's wisdom changed their lives. Some said it should be given with a warning that it will change your life! What follows are some of these lessons and some life-renewing prayers inspired by the angels, lending us the wisdom to heal the troubles of the heart and diseases in the body.

We greatly benefit when we allow the angels to intervene with God's Love, Light and Wisdom. Having a conscious relationship with the angels absolutely changes your life. The angels are gathering us together and sounding their trumpets. They celebrate uniting with us in a grand style. Sreper told me that there is a 'celebration all across Heaven when one on Earth decides to join with their angels.'

The angels are waiting. Accept that idea in your consciousness now. Ask for and receive their Divine guidance!

The angels are here to teach us how we can bring more love and joy into life. Let us be ready!

The focus should not be on the angels themselves but on the Light and Love they provide for us to see our way clearly. Sometimes healing is as simple as allowing a new idea to come into the mind that will open up a new possibility that hadn't been thought of before.

As the title implies, help is available to us all. It is in the first place we ought to look, but have often forgotten. Let this book reawaken that Divine Spark of Heavenly Light that God placed within all of us so long ago. There are no special dues, admission fees, or obligations.

All we have to do is ask. Ask for what is already ours by birthright and what God has indeed, already given each of us. We need only utter three little words to prompt His answer... *"Heaven help me!"*

And then listen for the angels to come rushing in.

Author's Notes

The angels refer to themselves as more than one being and never singularly. I have retained their writing style throughout the book, using "we" instead of "I" whenever they are referring to themselves. My own comments, as well as the questions asked, are italicized.

Also, in any reference made to God, I have used the traditional masculine pronoun for ease in writing. Please feel free to substitute whatever term for God you prefer.

♥

About Healing

"If we are willing to do the mental work,
almost anything can be healed." -Louise Hay

Over the years of communicating with Sreper and the Angels of the Great White Light, they have outlined various measures that we could take spiritually to aid in maintaining physical health and well-being. A theme emerged from listening to them, convincing me that we were created whole and perfect, just as God promised, and that we lacked nothing. But what did that mean? And why do we suffer with all this illness on Earth? Sreper repeatedly gave me messages such as what follows:

"Dear Ones, we say unto you, God's Will is for you to be well. Keep your heart clear and your intentions centered on maintaining good health, for whatever you set your sights on will manifest in physical form.

The Universal Law of Consciousness states that for as long as you have a physical body, that body can become ill, depending on where you place your personal beliefs and how you use the co-creative power given to you as your birthright from God. In its natural state, this power is neutral but it will take on whatever emotional charge you give it by your thoughts and beliefs. You were born into a body, into the physical universe to gain the experience of using this power to co-create with God. You and everyone else alive in the Earth is creating the mass consciousness experience, and although it may seem difficult for you to rise above this powerful belief system, (what we refer to as Earth's 'prevailing weather') it can be done by staying conscious of where you place your personal power.

1

Do you give it away to some person, place or thing that then controls you? We caution you to be vigilant, and keep watch over your thoughts, each and every one of them, for they are actually 'programming' what will happen to you and your body in the future. Disease and wellness comes not from outside yourself!

Believe in the God-like image in which He created you, that is, believe in complete wholeness, and regardless of disease on the planet, you will not become sick. Some people will get sick to get attention from their loved ones, to gain control over another, or to escape a situation, but we say you do not need to create an illness in order to accomplish some other goal!

All disease is caused by thoughts of disease. When you change disease thoughts to wellness thoughts, you also change the experience you will have. This will happen as soon as you are ready to do the inner work and are totally ready to release the need for disease. You start by becoming willing to learn the lesson the disease presents to you, and in doing so, the lesson is learned, the illness is released and peace, health and happiness prevails. Random bursts of joy can occur!

Dear Ones, we come into your lives at this time to encourage you to reach toward a more joyful goal. Set your sights higher! Set the pace for a new avenue of self-expression, for a future bright with dreams fulfilled. You are the leaders of this new wave of consciousness that is sweeping the planet, and along with it, a cleansing of hearts and minds of individuals everywhere shall take place. The journey appears difficult because you are the pioneers cutting a fresh new path through the forest, in charge of planting revolutionary light-filled thoughts in your world.

So, be brave and joyful 'warriors' on your journey. Ask

for our help and we will shower you with love, encouragement and sharper knives to cut away even more debris.

Your struggle is about to end, and it will end when you release the need for illness to manifest anywhere in your life or body. Be firm in your mind to rise above this learning, and you shall. You can do it, and you must do it, for it is God's Divine Law.

We hold the plan of Life to work out for all of you. It shall be on Earth as it is in Heaven – bright with glorious Light and without sickness anywhere. Treasure this thought with us, and carry it in your heart Dear Ones, and let us create a new Reality everyone wants to be alive in."

Q. What role do Guardian Angels play in our wellness prescription?

"Ask your angels for guidance and it is given you in the same way God says, seek and you will find. Call on us and we are at your side. We assist you in any and all goals wherein you ask for Light. We are ready to take you higher. We talk to you. We walk with you. We place highly creative, life-giving ideas in your mind. We open your heart to Love. We are patient and wait for you. We are here to let you know Love is a choice for you to make.

A few short years ago people were not as aware of their angels as they are now. We say that there has been much new awareness given us and we are pleased. There is a celebration all across Heaven when one in Earth joins with us.

There is a great new awakening sweeping through hearts and minds across the planet. We are now able to reach straight through the density of your realm and pull you up into a glorious state of being whenever you ask us to, and whenever you are ready. This is the role we play.

We invite you to call on us, but it is your choice which

way you will live your life. We wait by the side of the road until you call on us to unite your journey with ours."

Q. How does the healing process take place?

"We say unto you that we are the vibration of Love. Healing is inspired from the angels, as we emanate a higher, more refined energy from this Love that we are, that instills healing into whoever we touch, simply by touching them. This higher vibration, the speed at which this Light and Love energy radiates outwardly into the world of form, must heal simply because it is a higher vibration than the target it is aimed at.

This energy cannot be lowered to your density, but will always raise a lower vibration up to its level. This is what you call "healing," a raising of vibration. When a healing occurs, the lower vibration is actually swallowed up into the higher, faster one, and then it disappears, taking the physical manifestation of illness with it. In other words, the higher vibration will raise any lower vibration up to its level, thus healing and releasing it.

Darkness is lower in vibration than Light. *Illness IS darkness!* The act of extending healing from one being to another is an act of love, an act of sharing light and an act of healing."

Q. What can I do to help instill in others a zest for life?

"True teaching is always set by example. We say that in order to instill a zest for life, simply *be* a zest for life!"

Q. I am a health practitioner with a private practice. I hate to admit this but I have a fear of my patients getting well. I fear that could put me out of business because they will no longer need my services. Help!

4

"We say, release your fears and allow your clients to be healed. True, they shall be healed and may no longer need you to assist them, but you will then have a fresh batch of souls needing your help and guidance. They too, will heal and move on, but new patients will come to you to fill in the void. Allow the stream of clients to come and go and remove your fears from this.

Trust that God is the Source from which all blessings flow. He will continuously direct new clients to you."

Q. What can I do to assist the angels in my recovery process?

"First of all, we say to meditate daily at the same time of day or night, if possible, and call on your angels to bring you their vision. Adopt a meditation practice that suits you, for there are several methods to choose from, and it is very important that you enjoy this practice otherwise you may not follow it.

See yourself vibrantly alive and well. Through meditation, allow new awarenesses to enter your mind and heart. Be willing to let go of the past to clear the way for the new, and release what no longer serves your highest good to the Great White Light – even if you don't want to!

Ask for assistance if you need it. (Read "A Prayer At Daybreak," p. 171). We will lift your heart to the higher realms of love and forgiveness, and give you peace and new life, if you but ask.

Exercise kindness to yourself and get involved in activities that bring you joy. Say no to people and practices that bring you down, or elicit painful memories.

Take a hands-on, active approach in your healing process. Put yourself in the midst of people who love and support you and what you are doing. Be careful not to share with those who would laugh at, or ridicule your recovery. Stay in the mental presence of what it is you wish to accomplish and let go of those who do not have your highest and best interests at heart. *Remember, you are in process!*

Life may be confusing for a little while. Things are constantly changing and there is a great transformation taking place within you now. Simply be with it.

All things happen for good. You will notice changes in your outer world too. Be aware of all of this and keep your eyes on the goal. You shall, indeed emerge a new person – like a butterfly from a cocoon – with ravishing beauty and ready to fly."

Q. Where are the angels when a healing has been asked for, but the person does not get well?

"We say unto you do not judge what occurs in the physical for you cannot see the entire picture from the tiny portal through which you look. Sometimes the reason a person may not heal is because his life on Earth is complete, his mission has been accomplished.

Always, always remember there are no accidents and nothing happens that isn't supposed to happen. This means that no one dies a second sooner than he is supposed to, according to the Divine Plan. When you ask for healing, put in your mind that your words serve as actual prayer treatments. Your words are powerful! These new healing words soften the human condition and create a renewed heart in the person. When we speak of 'heart' we do not necessarily mean the physical heart, but instead we refer to that part of you that is real and lives forever, beyond the physical body.

The Earth plane is like a school house for you. It has been setup by your higher self for you to experience the entire spectrum of feelings and emotions. Remember, that you are not without power on that plane. Your words are your power. Believe in them. Believe in yourself!

Ask for healing and healing is given to you, but be aware that you cannot know when or in which way the angels bring it to you. Know that it will come to benefit you in the highest way possible.

In some cases, physical death may be the cure. Your human sight and knowledge are cloaked in darkness and you cannot see the entire picture. Remember, your guardian angels never leave their post. We keep an eye on you and on what is God's Divine Will for you. We see the path you're on and we know the goals you've chosen. We guide you in making any adjustments along the way, if you so ask, but we will never step in and take control. We may nudge you, or persuade you to change the course you're on in order to divert any unnecessary or painful experience.

This is precisely why we ask you to turn within and listen to your inner voice. We are there loving you and coaching you. We are always there. It is our wish to alleviate the pain humanity feels it must endure for lack of having more enlightened choices.

We say unto you, nourish your goal of being healed. Imagine all the cells in your body are radiantly alive and in constant motion of creating new cells and new life in you. Bring your fragmented pieces back together and see yourself whole once again. Know the Light of a new day has come, and along with it an angel, your Guardian Angel, who gently knocks upon your door and asks to be let in. We standby ready to serve you and God, according to His Will."

7

Accidents and Injuries

"Men occasionally stumble on the truth, but most of them pick themselves up and hurry off as if nothing had happened."
-Sir Winston Churchill

Q. I have had many accidents in my life. Why? And what lesson am I to learn from being crippled?

"We see you have greatly resisted learning your lessons in Earth school. Your soul, however, has an agenda of its own to awaken you from your 'self-inflicted darkness.' It is your soul calling to you to snap out of the belief – and out of your drama – that says you must injure yourself in order to be loved, or that you must suffer in order to be 'saved.'

Nonsense! We say it is time for you to wake up and accept God's reality for you. Something has shifted inside of you and stirred you to find the truth. You come to us now to have this awakening. Your soul has asked for you to be released from this cycle of injury and pain. Your soul has been calling you to wake up from your ancient belief in sacrifice, and to – literally – rise up and walk!

Let us enlighten you. You believed that in order 'to be saved' you had to give up something you valued. Remember the origin of this belief, for therein is your release from it. Your answer lies in your prayer. Ask, and it is opened unto you. Seek and you shall find. Your healing shall take place as soon as you are ready in consciousness to accept God's peace, love and healing.

Fear not that you shall walk again. Do not give your power to those who say walking again is impossible, for we say there is a much greater power in God! Place your power there! Love yourself enough to forgive yourself of the idea of sacrifice and that somehow God would allow you to suffer. He did not create suffering. You did.

Dear one, awaken from your dream and allow God's Light to enter and do its healing work. Be not surprised that you shall walk again.

Know that what has been asked in your heart, has also been answered. Think only the new thoughts that come to you now from on High – from your Father who is in Heaven – for His words are what will heal you."

Addiction

"There is a principle which is a bar against all information,
which is proof against all arguments and which cannot fail to keep
a man in everlasting ignorance - that principle is contempt prior
to investigation." -Herbert Spencer, A.A. "Big Book"

*Q. Sreper, what could possibly be the reason behind
people experiencing painful addictions to alcohol and other
substances? What is the significance of the 12-Steps in the
recovery process?*

"We say unto you, the key is in remembering who you
are. You are spirit – a spark of God – inhabiting a physical
body to experience life on Earth. We are here to bring Light
to your path of *recovery*, which really means *discovery* of
your soul. We remind you that you are always exactly perfect wherever you are in this unfolding process. You are
always exactly where you find yourself for a very good reason. Addiction to drugs, alcohol, or other substances is seen
as the physical manifestation of your soul's desire to learn
and gain a complete education – indeed, a vast learning of
an entire array of feelings and emotions are available for
you to learn while on Earth. There is no other place in the
universe that offers such a curriculum.

When you do not understand why something happens to
you, or why you are experiencing pain, loss, or suffering,
remember that it is a lesson for you, devised by your Higher Self for your soul's growth. It is also the desire of your
soul to choose a higher path with regards to your life situations, that is, to move through your curriculum with ease...
and with joy. *Yes, joy!* God did not create pain for you to
experience, nor should you, for you and He are cut from the
same cloth. God did not place you on Earth to be powerless
and out of touch with Him. It is pain, now, that calls to you

and asks you to remember who you are.

Dear One, you are a Child of God, a Divine Aspect of your Creator, a thread in His radiant tapestry of Love and Light – each and every one of you. Your light is dim perhaps from forgetfulness, but this is a call for you to come home to ignite your radiance.

God, in His loving kindness, gave you your perfect place, known to you in Christian terms as 'Heaven,' in which to abide. You decided, however, to experience something other than what He has given you, thereby creating the dimension in which you find yourselves. In your evolutionary process, you have forgotten who you really are and that you decided to live apart from your Divine Heritage.

And because you have asked, we intervene now and invite you to come home. Remember that you are co-creators of your experience in the world, and you are not without help to transform what you see into the blessing it really is. We say to keep watch over your thoughts and stay conscious of what you allow into your co-creative process. You are powerful beings. You have created what it is you see in your world and we say you have the same power to recreate what you would rather have. If you are experiencing anything less than joy in your life, choose again. See the larger picture before you. See as God sees! Redirect your focus and redirect your life.

We offer you fresh, new ideas for you to consider. The Creator made you in His image and likeness, meaning that you hold in your hand His creative power. You have the inherent ability of creating joyous lives, for that is what God gave you. Heaven is your birthright! We see that you have instead created pain and suffering, believing somehow that this is what you deserved. In you is an emptiness, a hole in your energy field, caused from your amnesia and you have tried to fill this void by your habitual consumption of alcohol, drugs, or other substances. Have you ever wondered why they call alcohol 'spirits?' We say it is because you have forgotten your 'spiritual connection' and have instead turned your focus to physical means to get back what you felt you'd lost – to fill up what was an imminent, empty wound. In the process, you lost your way.

We say unto you, you have simply misplaced your personal power which shall not continue once you decide that you've had enough pain and suffering from the addiction that has been governing you. In your decision to recover your true spirit, the God-Spark, a new Light comes to you and shines clearly and brightly. It promises you will not lose your way again. By remembering that you are a thread in the Creator's glorious tapestry of Light, an aspect of the Divine, the spaces that were once filled with substances will be filled again with *you* as you were meant to be, rendering you complete and no longer in an endless search of something else to fill you up.

Addiction to drugs and alcohol is an escape regardless of the many forms it takes on. Many die trying to attain rest from addiction. They refused to hear their inner voice calling them home to their Higher State of being.

Pain is a great teacher on the Earth plane. Listen to its message, for in it is your true escape to the higher reality and spiritual understanding.

You thought there was something outside of you – a substance – that would relieve your pain and suffering, but we say the only cure is a Divine shift in consciousness. The key to this door is within you now. This is what will create a new reality in you and in your world. No longer will you need to search for something else, for you will be complete and will remember your completeness, just as God had planned. To those of you who are in recovery, do you know how fortunate you are to be awakening to your soul's deepest desire? If this statement makes you angry at your life, we ask you to take the time to uncover who you really are. Go deep within yourself. Ask for your guardian angel to be with you, to guide you, and we will walk beside you on the path to Heaven.

Go beneath the chemical clothes you have been wearing, the ones that have covered up the real you - for they have also covered your Light. What you have been seeking in the outer world of form through your addiction, had long ago been placed within you where it remains forever untouched. You have simply buried it.

In your terms, the 12-step program is a spiritual process, an unfolding of your soul's highest will for you, speaking to you in terms your human mind can grasp, then gently takes you higher. Remember, everything in your world has roots deep in the spiritual realms. You are, and have always been, spiritual beings who have been residing in a physical world. Coming into (12-Step) recovery is but your call to awaken and remember who you are beneath the lampshade.

Call your power home to your heart, Dear Ones. See this as part of a grand plan that your soul has chosen for you to awaken. Addiction is your call to come home, your call to come home to know your true self and to release the need for needing something outside of yourself to alter you, to fill you up, or to bring you joy. You only need yourself, the self who is already whole, perfect and complete, as you were created to be. Nothing can alter that – thank Heaven! You only thought something could."

Q. Why do people become addicted to substances such as drugs and alcohol?

"It is a fear of life that causes a person to become addicted and we say unto you that there isn't anything to fear but your own imagination. We suggest you embrace life – *all of life*. We see a familiar pattern for addiction is that of running and hiding from what you perceive as fear.

At this present time we say you have forgotten what it is you are running from. You fear, fear! Upon arrival in human form, you dreaded the task of living, and sought escape from it. To release yourself from this cycle you turned to using and depending on alcohol.

We dare say unto you that your fear is not real, and there is nothing to fear but this imagination of yours. Your lesson is to embrace life. In doing so, you access inner peace and are blessed with God's Divine Grace to live a happy life."

Q. How can I permanently recover from my addiction?

"You may permanently recover by choosing to live your life rather than trying to escape from it! You will permanently recover when you decide that you want to experience life and reap life's rich rewards without the use of any life-enhancers, such as drugs and alcohol.

Plant the seed of renewal and life purpose in your heart today and reap its reward later. Know that your life is full of meaning and is in no way a wasted life as you once believed. You have life because God gave you life. Yes, miracles do happen! You are clearing away the fog and cutting a new path. This moment is a brand new start for you, if you so choose. You are a beautiful, vibrant soul underneath those chemical clothes, eager with anticipation to break through the fog of addiction... just like the sun bursts through the clouds after a heavy rainfall."

Q. Is my husband capable of having joyful sobriety?

"Yes, but we say you must release your focus on him and turn it onto yourself. As you grow and change, you shall see your life differently and your situation with him differently. Change the film in the projector and you change the movie you are watching."

Q. Will we be spiritually and financially successful after recovery?

"It is quite a difficult thing for angels to measure value and success, for we have a different perspective than you. If you have made up your mind and have set your intention on coming through the fear of fear, and break through the fog of addiction, then you cannot fail but to accomplish your dreams. It doesn't look easy from where you are because you haven't yet decided to make it easy.

We are also here to tell you to choose grace and ease in your letting go of addiction. Ask for the strength to endure this passageway and for the ability to see yourself free from all addictions and as happy. Yes, it is this simple if you will but allow yourself to see the simplicity. This need not be hard to do!

Ask, and you have the Angels of Heaven holding you as you make your way through this change. A new perspective makes all the difference, so ask us to show you a picture of what your new life could look like now. Your life will be full from that point of decision on, and we say, you shall enjoy every minute of it. Believe it, and remember that we walk beside you with every step.

Choose life and the habits that support life, and you will see only *life!*"

Aging Process

Q. I am showing signs of aging. I feel as though my body is falling apart! I have pain in my teeth and gums, and my hair is falling out. Help!

"Your teeth and gums are giving you problems due to a long-held behavior called stubbornness, which in turn causes indecisiveness. Your teeth represent decisiveness and teeth problems represent indecisiveness. Gums represent the seat of stubbornness. Your toes ache and give you problems because of your fear of moving forward with your life. When one does not choose to go forward in their life, the body will deliver a such messages to you.

Loss of hair comes from another tightly held belief that somehow your manliness, your strength of character, is represented in your hair, but we say it is fear and tension causing you to hang on to life so tightly, trying to control it rather than allowing it to flow through you. You feel that along with the aging process, certain changes must happen in the physical body.

The lesson here is to blossom with ease and grace and enjoy all aspects of your life – at every age level – for there is beauty in each and every one of them. Focus on agelessness knowing that whatever you focus on you create."

Allergies

"As a Child of God I am sensitive only to God
and only Him will I serve." -Cushing Smith

Q. Sreper, why do people suffer from allergies?

"We say that from time-to-time, your traveling clothes (physical bodies) can gather some dust. You are not on Earth to be afraid to live, so kick up your heels and create! Don't stand by cautiously in the sandbox watching others play in the clay. Grab your toys and dig in.

In your meditations, ask to have your angels come and dust you off. Be assured your wings will carry you to new heights of glory and safety. Let go of the dusty old reins tied to false gods and face the Light. Recreate a new experience of life, now. You need not make any major life-changing decisions, or throw anyone out of your life. We would rather you drop the resistance and suggest you welcome them into your new life. We dare say that you are not really allergic to anything. You are sensitive and this sensitivity has manifested in you because you have resisted life and have been afraid of its glorious experiences. In suppressing what you came to Earth to learn, you have unknowingly created allergic reactions to the environment around you. Blame and guilt must manifest somewhere!

We say to you who suffer from allergies, you have been afraid to live. You never felt completely at home on Earth, and it is time to give this gift to yourself.

Breathe in all of life! You hesitate to function fully on Earth because of a fear that it is not 'safe' to be on Earth. We say to you in order to be healed you need to release this fear. If you are not aware of what these fears are, we say you really need not define them or give them any more power, but simply ask God to remove them.

Learn to embrace all of life. Welcome yourself to the world! Give the world a big hug, mentally, upon awakening each morning. Give yourself a hug! Become fully alive within your world and within your body. Become enthused about life. Discover what interests you and then do it. Create fun. You do not need to stay in the same place forever. Go on an adventure. Do new things. Go to new places. See new people. Read new books. Create newness and leave old, dusty things behind.

Clean your closets. Go through your possessions and let go of things you haven't used in a year and will never use again. Either throw them to the trash pile, or give them away to someone who will use them. Do this now and do it every time the seasons change. This will clear all your passageways, your sinuses on the physical, as well as the etheric and emotional passageways. Get new life moving!

This is a call to simply awaken to your heart now, for it is calling you home to your natural state of good health. Call on the angels and we will guide your life, and when your heart is filled with only Love and Light, your aches and your allergies will dissolve into nothing."

Anger

"Most people are willing to change, not because they see the light, but because they feel the heat." -Unknown

Q. Sreper, what is the best way to handle difficult, controlling people so as to heal anger and return to peace?

"Dear Ones, we see the human plane in a much different light than you and ask in these moments when your peace is disturbed, for you to see the higher purpose behind what is going on. Even if you cannot see it, ask and we can open the shutters and give you light on what troubles you.

The Earth school experience has been setup by you to learn the path of the heart. Your task is to undo the ego and what it has created and made real, for it is nothing more than a trickster gaining power from your misdirected thought. When you feel you've had enough pain and want peace instead of what you created, release the hold the ego has on you, or the hold you believe it has on you. We urge you to step into the lesson the ego has set up for you, and release it. This is easier to do than you know. Make the decision and then ask for assistance. We can help you see options and choose differently.

Instead of seeing a person as controlling and manipulative, see them as crying out for love. You need not do anything but send love to the situation. Then, be patient and observe what develops next. Maybe this situation was setup by the universe to get you to let go of something you no longer need. Perhaps the thing someone is trying to get from you is blocking good from coming to you! This could just be a drama being acted out in order to allow an even greater gift to flow into your life! Do not forget that all things work together for good, no matter what your vantage point or opinion is.

Whenever your ego judges someone else, or their motives, tell yourself this is a sign for you to go within and see yourself there. Where are you not trusting? Where have you been manipulative or afraid? And regardless of what is discovered, send love to the situation. Muster up your compassion. Show understanding. Even if you cannot possibly see a reason for their behavior, trust that it is part of a bigger plan that is birthing yet a greater good somewhere in consciousness."

Q. What can I do about my anger?

"If you are angry, ask the angels who love you dearly, to remove your anger. Ask them to remove your bitterness and your resentment. If asking them is difficult for you to do, we ask why do you choose to hold onto something that hurts you when you could be free of it and have peace instead? Do not pass judgment on anyone for this opens the floodgate for others to judge you. Indeed, we say, let the one who is without judgment cast the first stone.

If you become judgmental, ask the angels to remove your criticisms. Ask for peace and love to fill the empty space. Always hold the highest truth possible in your heart and mind – for yourself and for those who are in your life with you. If you do not know what this is, or how to do this, ask that the path be shown to you to open your heart.

Ask and receive. Create even the slightest of openings... a laser light piercing the darkness of anger... and hold those you are angry at, in peace and love. Ask your angels to escort you to higher levels of seeing your life, and we will. Be open to let go of your anger for this brings you the peace you long for. Look only to peaceful resolutions to your conflicts, and we promise, you shall see only peace.

We love you and await your call to open to and accept

our love and guidance. Your job is to take that one tiny step toward Heaven. Sadness and negativity doesn't exist here. Make the choice to leave anger behind you and you will arrive at the place of Love that your heart remembers."

A Prayer to Release Anger

"Father, come sit with me for a moment. I am angry and I need to see as you see, right now, and to trust in my heart that You are working your magic in this situation. Please let me be free of this frightening emotion. Give me the strength to let go and let You step in to fix what is wrong.

Until I can see this clearly, guide me so I do not hurt myself or anyone else by my thoughts, words or deeds. God, lift me up and free me. Amen."

Animal Cruelty

"What counts is not necessarily the size of the dog in the fight -
it's the size of the fight in the dog." -Dwight D. Eisenhower

Q. Sreper, animals are suffering at the hands of humans which is absolutely infuriating! What is the reason for this senselessness?

"You must understand that in the world of duality there are many seeming injustices that will never make sense to you on that level. Also, please know that nothing goes unnoticed on your plane, for it is all a part of God's Great Plan. The animal kingdom has come into third dimension as a gift to humankind. They know that their part of the plan is to teach human beings unconditional love. This lesson seems harsh and cruel to you because you only see the physical aspect of this divine exchange between your kingdoms. If you judge an animal as suffering, we assure you the nature spirit in charge of that animal prepares it for his departure from that plane. They know what they are doing. In most cases, the animal's spirit has left its physical body before feeling much pain. It is Divine Law that animals will not suffer in death. In cases where you hear an animal yelp, it simply is a wake-up call and a lesson in compassion for the one who comes to care for it.

There are no accidents, and all things work together for good. There are no sacrifices and no animal's life is 'wasted.' We suggest that you not focus on the suffering, but see only the gift the animals give to you. Love is released from your heart to them, and alas, their "suffering" has not been in vain, but has been fulfilled, for you have learned compassion. Do not refuse the gift, Dear Ones, for that is the Gold the animals give you."

Arthritis

"Kites rise highest against the wind; not with it."
-Sir Winston Churchill

Q. Why do people develop painful arthritic conditions?

"We say, a person develops arthritis due to several different thought patterns he or she holds in their mind as their truth. They often believe they will develop arthritis because it is seen as running through their family's hereditary structures. They have not fully realized that they do not need to accept an illness, or any kind of limitation, for that matter. Each individual is free to think and believe differently than what they had been previously taught. We say, the only thing that is hereditary is the thought or belief system that is handed down from generation to generation.

At this time on Earth, it is widely accepted that pain is the greatest teacher. Pain gets your attention! You do not willingly make certain changes in your body or your life without something calling to get your attention first. It is then that you decide something is wrong and must be fixed. Understand that we are not condemning this sequence of actions, not at all, for that is simply where your present consciousness is.

What is needed is for you to let go of the idea that you need pain to be your teacher. Become willing, in this very moment, to forgive yourself of all your past, allowing yourself to be free to live life new right here and right now. This means be kind and loving to yourself. Release all old ideas that keep you stuck in self-judgment and self-criticism. Your Father has already forgiven any self-perceived wrong doing that may have occurred since the beginning of time. Yet, you have not forgiven yourself.

We say unto you, stop the defiance. Stop holding yourself in such limitation, and in such rigid patterns, for there is more life waiting to come into your experience if you would but welcome each new experience with an open heart and mind. Rather than dread anything new, we suggest you anticipate with joy the good in every situation and your lives would accelerate into much higher levels. We say unto you, be ready for change. Show signs of life! Know that with each new day that dawns upon the Earth, there is also a great new good awaiting, like buried treasure waiting to be discovered. Be exuberant!

Release your past and let free yourself from the arthritic prison. If you cannot see how this step can be taken, we suggest you ask for just a little bit of willingness to see your situation differently, and this willingness will give you the strength you need. Go forward now, knowing you are blessed and carry with you the keys to a healthy new body."

Birth Control
Methods of Abortion and Adoption
"Life is what happens to us while we're making other plans."
-John Lennon

Q. Sreper, would you enlighten us about abortion?

"We say that the abortion issue could be one of the hottest debates facing humanity. We would like to dispel the incorrect myths that people hold as truth regarding this, but we wonder, will we be heard? Let us begin by saying that there are never any accidents in the consciousness that creates your Earthly experience.

Each and every individual soul decides what kind of experience it will have in the upcoming lifetime. And, we add, that every single experience happens for a very good reason; it is Divine orchestration. Do not sit in judgment over this for we say there have been times you have enrolled into this same school of learning. In this debate let us say this... a soul may decide to experience Earth's density for only a brief period of time, and no longer. They choose not to have a long lifetime for a myriad of reasons. Incoming souls may also choose to be the bearer of a lesson to the parents whose souls have asked to learn something valuable without the lesson spanning an entire lifetime.

Another possibility is that the parents have chosen to experience grief and loss through 'losing' a baby. But note, the baby is also a soul gaining his or her own lessons in this experience. Often we see that this is what the parent's souls have picked for developing a stronger bond of love for each other. You see, Dear Ones, babies bring a very special gift to their parents. Their goal is love, and only love.

We say unto you that there are many, many variables in the abortion issue and each situation should be read separately as each would reveal a different story. But we say, there is no 'murder' taking place. No one is 'killing' anyone. All that happens is done according to an agreement between the souls involved before birth. What you see are lessons being acted out, if you will. We cannot say this enough, but those of you who have trouble over this debate need to stop judging, for what is really at issue is this: There is one group of souls trying to control another group of souls. Period.

We say that if it were not this debate on abortion, these souls would wield their power over something else! This issue is about control over human rights and it is not about abortion directly. We suggest you not create any karma over this. Do not hold judgment with what others do in their lives, for we remind you that you have no idea what their soul's path is.

Bless and release to your angels anything you do not understand. Allow us to answer your troubled mind. Allow the Divine to intervene and instill peace in your heart. All of you are God's children! You are all equal.

We say there are a few things on Earth that are nearly impossible for you to truly understand with your limited vantage point, as it were, so we ask that you trust what we say, for our view is higher and we see the Divine outworking in all situations. We say that even the starving children in the world are learning lessons their souls have devised. Painful for you to watch, yes, we agree, but it is their free will choice.

We suggest that you pray for enlightenment for all souls, Dear Ones, and trust God's Plan. Trust there is a reason and get on with the business of living your life. Open your heart and release whatever you do not understand to God who heals all things if you but allow Him to. Let not your hearts and minds be troubled, but let the healing begin now. And so it is!"

Q. Why can't I get pregnant?

"We see that you want a baby girl so much, that you actually fear you could have a boy. This is what is preventing you from becoming pregnant. We say to you that this dynamic will not change until you are able to open your heart to love's gift and accept either one."

Q. Would adopting a child upset our family unit?

"You have been unsuccessful in adopting because of your haunting indecision. The universe loves a made-up mind! It does not know how to answer you when you are 'wishy-washy.' Actually, a child would bring much joy into your life. It would also pose some major adjustments, to be sure. You have a lot of fear surrounding this decision. You haven't been entirely decided in your mind that you want a child or you would have adopted a child already. You fear disruption of your family. You fear you cannot get the baby girl you want. You fear if you adopt a foreign girl she won't be healthy, and that, too, would disrupt your picture of a perfect family.

We ask you to take another look at your situation from a higher point of view, if you will, to see as we see. Ask yourself, 'Are not all children beautiful? Doesn't everyone have a unique purpose here? Doesn't everyone have an equal right to their own learning experience?'

Realize that you cannot make a mistake in your selection process, for it is a part of your learning experience. Do you know that if you fear adopting an unhealthy child, that you may, through your fear draw an unhealthy child to you?

We do not mean to add stress to your decision process

by adding more questions, we only mean to enlighten this issue for you so you will make a clearer choice. Rather than being fearful of adopting the 'wrong' baby, believe you are divinely guided to the 'right' baby. Know in your heart there can be no mistake made. Ask to be guided in your search and know in your heart that your child also finds you. Listen to your heart and your fears fall silent.

Creation smiles on you as you take on such a task as loving and nurturing someone else's child. We suggest you let this love guide you all through your life, and the world will respond to such a loving gesture in kind. You can never lose by operating your life from Love and you will never be disappointed."

Q. Sreper, what do you suggest for a method of birth control?

"We say unto you that birth control is so very simple you may laugh out loud at its simplicity, but hear our words. Say unto the kingdom of yourself, to your higher self, exactly what it is you want.

Just speak the words! Say, 'I do not want to give birth to any child at this time. So be it. Amen.' You are free to change your mind at a later date. Stay conscious of what you want in your life and pray that plan.

We feel your argument that method of birth control cannot be that simple, but we say to you that this turns into doubt regarding the absolute power of your own words. We suggest that until you trust your words, and know with certainty you are the master of your reality, continue to use some physical form of birth control."

Busy-ness
"Too many times we confuse motion with progress." -Cyclops

Q. What is with all the busy-ness here on Earth? People are too busy to do things, even the things we need to do in our daily lives. How can we let go and relax when so much is clamoring in our heads?

"We see that you have been too busy to even talk with us! Let us start by saying that there is plenty of time to accomplish all that you need to accomplish. What is lacking is trust in the perfect outworking of life. We see that you scurry from place to place and from project to project, and whether you realize it or not, all along you are doing exactly what your life purpose is! All the errands, all the interruptions, they all hold potential learning in them, some great and some small.

What we suggest you do is take on a new energy, a new attitude about this and about how, and at what speed, life unfolds itself to you. You must get it into your mind and heart that your life cannot go without you. In the 'franticness of your busy-ness,' you fear time will run out before you get everything done. We say unto you that time and life will not run out. No alarm clock is set to go off somewhere and no one is calling you home until it is time for you to go home. The goals on Earth are not necessarily to get things done but to garner knowledge from the things that unfold in the process of getting them done. That is where the learning and the glory are.

We remind you that you are not on Earth to run a race. Yes, things can get hectic and pull you off your center, but that happens only when you allow it. We say unto you that you, and no one else, is in control of your life unless, of course, you have placed your power elsewhere. If you are easily pulled away from where your soul purpose leads you, we suggest that you pause for a moment.

Before your feet hit the ground running tomorrow morning, quiet your mind. Empty it completely. Tell your worries that you will tend to them later, but you are calling a time-out. Relax and know in the moment you are gathering your life-force together with your purpose for that day only, and not for your entire lifetime. Rest knowing you are safe. There is no other place you need to be this moment. Allow a flood of comfort from Heaven to come over you like a warm quilt.

Breathe.

Now, take another moment and envision a day spent with your angels. What would that be like? What would you do? How could this day be different than the ones that have gone before it? What would you ask your angels to assist you with? What would you like your relationship with them to be like? What would you ask them?

Notice how you are feeling. Take a few minutes to feel deeply, to connect to the sizzling and sparkling energy of Heaven itself. Know your prayer is heard. Open the door inside your heart/mind and let Heaven in. We not only will be there to assist you and make your day go smoothly, but we are there already to guide peace into physical reality and to bring you your highest good.

All you need to do is clear yourself and accept what we offer you. Trust that your divine purpose is unfolding to you and to the world. Allow us to elevate your thinking to see as we see, and to know that all things happen for your ultimate good."

Career and Life Path Decisions

"Do not follow where the path may lead.
Go instead where there is no path and leave a trail." -Muriel Strode

Q. Sreper, I have a fear my career is going nowhere. What can you tell me to help me relax and let go of this concern?

"Dear Ones, we assure you that career opportunities unfold to you in the exact moment you are ready to receive them. We ask you to release any fear you have about this and focus your attention instead on appreciating what you have right now in this moment.

Bless your job regardless of its rewards. Bless it especially if you loathe doing it. We suggest that you, indeed bless everything in sight. Thank spirit for the wonderful gifts you have already received, for a grateful heart is open and willing to receive even more!

Keep your focus on the Light that you are and guard yourself from nursing negativity. As appreciation takes root in your heart, more opportunities will abound in your life. No one is attracted to you or what you have to offer if you are in fear.

Keep yourself attuned to daily plans and to what is happening right now rather than leaving yourself open to future plans that are too far from you to have any control over. Focus your mind on appreciation and allow that Light to grow in you."

Q. Sreper, will I be doing more Lightwork or something else? I am willing if it is what Divine Will is for me.

"Now your true life work begins. Your Light shines as far as we can see, all across Heaven and Earth, and it cannot be contained under the ego's lampshade any longer.

Become willing and available for us to serve through you.

It is time to go to the next step. In faith, we say take this leap and your wings shall flap and you shall fly!"

Q. I owe my parents a lot of money for sending me through college. What can I do to improve my financial situation and pay them back?

"We say unto you that in the action of following your bliss, which lies within every human heart, however deep it is buried, the soul discovers its ultimate purpose for incarnating on Earth. If you so choose, you will make your living doing what you love. It is your choice. The God of your understanding provides for you as He has always provided for you.

We say to you that it was your parent's choice to help you financially, for it made them feel good and useful on your journey. Accept their help graciously, and take the burden off of you. Divine timing will make it possible for you to repay those you are indebted to, but show your gratitude rather than subservient attitude, for that will uplift everyone involved. If you focus on the burden, your light is dim and helps no one.

Tell your parents that you deeply appreciate their kindness and their support. Tell them you plan to repay the debt as soon as you are able to. They will love your forthright honesty. It will warm their hearts to know you appreciate their help and care about your responsibility. Such few words can make a big difference! One can't possibly think clearly when worried over something else so, we say take the added stress off of yourself so you can become clear as to what direction you want to move into.

Follow what you want to do and do that which is written in your heart. You shall get support and accomplish the reasons why you incarnated on Earth in the first place. This is all a part of a plan to help your soul learn to trust in Divine guidance and later, to teach this to others. Ask that you be guided as you approach the new doors ahead in the hallway of the school of life and the unseen forces of good shall be there to open them with you. Be good to yourself and walk on the highest road possible."

Q. The corporate world isn't where I want to be any longer. What do you suggest I do?

"First of all, celebrate your awakening, for hearing the call to follow your heart. You have just awakened from a long sleep. You have just shut off the alarm clock and are rubbing the sleep from their eyes. You're still a bit groggy and don't quite know where you are, or what day it is, but you are about to step from that old bed and into something new and alive.

This is not something to cause alarm. This is simply what change looks and feels like. Give yourself the courage to move through this change and indeed, to celebrate it! Be good to yourself for you've come a long way. You are awake and alive, and what you are shedding is no longer serving your highest good. We say, let it pass.

Ask yourself what career would bring you joy? Reach deep within your heart and ask what makes you feel the happiest and most fulfilled. Become clear on what you really want and chart the route to get there. Next, take these new awarenesses, these pieces of information you receive and blend them all together. You will probably find that you are already headed in your chosen direction, but have been temporarily side-tracked due to indecisiveness and, perhaps from comparing yourself to others. Honor yourself for having come through the foggy night of change, from the corporate world to your own field of dreams.

And now in the morning light the sun is burning off the mist, leaving the horizon clear for you to see your way."

Q. What is my life's task and how does it relate to my career?

"Do you realize that the reasons you walk on the planet have little or nothing to do with what job you fill? We say that it is most important that you understand this. Look deep within yourself and let your heart speak to you very honestly. Ask what you would love to do if you had but a day to live? What would you do? How would you choose to spend this time?

Your life's task, Dear One, has been to do one thing and that is to consciously connect with the Divine within you. The rest of life is just a lesson, props, if you will, to bring you the lesson of connecting your conscious mind to God once again. Open your heart to hearing *its* voice and follow through with what it asks you to do. Open to its voice and follow it. Ask and receive. Your heart will never mislead you. It knows the way you want to go."

For years I struggled with my life purpose and what work I was on Earth to accomplish. So have most people I know. From age 10 I knew I wanted to be an interior designer or architect, working to help people create beautiful environments in which to live and work. At age 20, I went to college to study interior design.

Soon after graduation I went into disillusionment while in my first job. I worked as an assistant to an interior designer, doing what I thought I would do for the rest of my life. But I was not happy. There was something significant missing. Looking back at that time now, I see that I was a spiritual babe in the woods and needed to really find myself, to follow my soul's purpose rather than walk in the world my ego had created. Wherever I turned in the outer world to fulfill that dream of being an interior designer, I was stopped. I either didn't get the jobs, or I was terminated soon after. I prayed to know my life purpose and it eventually unfolded to me as I was ready to step into those shoes. Helping people heal spiritually meant more to me than anything else, and the Universe saw a way in which I was to serve. Now, 25 years later I have become a Feng Shui practitioner. Feng Shui is the ancient Chinese secret I had sought all my life. It is the art of placement of all our possessions to best enhance various aspects of our life. For short, Feng Shui is the application of environmental affirmations that work to heal the lives of those who live in the space. It was the missing piece!

In Feng Shui we eliminate from our lives the things that no longer serve a purpose, that no longer make our hearts sing. Allow spirit to move through you in such a way as to deepen your sense of knowing your life mission and to bring you resolution concerning your career path. Be at peace knowing you are perfectly placed at all times. This inner peace shall always lead you where you need to be tomorrow. Delight in trusting that God really does know best. If a job suddenly ends, take heart it is because there is something far greater coming.

Q. Help me! Which career should I pursue?
"Dear Ones, we say you are not on Earth to work at a

job, but to accomplish the goals written across your heart. The job you take, or the career you choose are simply ways in which certain teachings are presented to you to learn on Earth. They are props in the human play.

We suggest you quiet your conscious mind and become perfectly clear. Ask yourself these questions. What would you absolutely love to do? Why are you not doing it? What are you afraid of? Herein, will be the answer you seek.

You don't yet realize that the entire world waits for you to manifest what is before you to create on Earth. The plan was already set in motion before you were born. You are the only one blocking your career. This keeps your life's plan in a holding pattern and keeps it there until you let go of the fears.

We say, you do not have to sacrifice anything to gain something else. Taste all of what life has given you. Don't be so harsh on yourself from trying one career and then another. Be kind to yourself and extend this kindness to others, for that is the truest accomplishment you can learn on Earth. Practice this in whatever career you choose."

Q. I live in the middle of nowhere and not much is available for jobs. Should I move to a place where there are better opportunities to make a living?

"When a heart is open and truly ready for something to begin, it matters not where you live, for that particular thing will be attracted to you just as metal shavings are to a magnet. Simply be open. Ready yourself to accept greater possibilities. You do not know the ways in which the universe works to bring good to you. It will always find you no matter where you live and what you do, because, you create it by your own consciousness.

The only rule is to do what produces joy in your heart.

Wherever you go, wherever you work and whatever you do, you always bring your own consciousness to the workplace. If happiness in your work is what you seek, become happy doing your work. If joy is what you seek, become more joyful. Whatever you have in your consciousness is what will be created in all the outer circumstances in your life.

What you give is what will ultimately be reflected back to you. That is why we say to set new goals higher than you have before. Follow your heart in all your decisions, for with a heart open to the winds of change, the right work at the right pay will surely materialize."

Affirmation for Ease and Grace in My Work

"I work at a comfortable and healthy pace. All my chores are completed on time and with ease. I bring people into my life who love what I do and who support me and my life purpose.

For my friends and work associates, I choose people who radiate love, warmth and joy, releasing from my life anything less than that now. So be it. Amen."

Q. I need a creative outlet and my friends are encouraging me to take up singing. Although the lessons are expensive, is this a worthwhile venture for me?

"We say unto you, there is nothing more important than doing what you love. Do the things that bring the greatest joy to your heart, for when you do, you are accomplishing what it is you came to Earth to do. Contemplate the gifts that have been given you to use. Sing and dance if those are your talents. Follow your heart. Do not listen to what the world dictates you should do, for you are on Earth to write your own script. Give your dreams a chance. In them you will find peace and happiness. All the things you have done so far have led up to where you are now, where we encourage you to take a leap in faith. We dare say you shall come out of this dirge singing! Allow the universe to support the dreams it has planted in you, and the world awaits its fulfillment and its glory in you. Simply give yourself permission to have the experience. Seek not outside of yourself for who you are, for remember, the pearl lies *inside* the shell.

We remind you you are not on Earth to become anything more than you already are. You merely came to express who you are. The Creator has given you the choice to do what you love and we suggest that you do it with passion. We say, as you discover who that wonderful person is inside, you shall also discover what it is that brings you joy in your work.

Celebrate your waking up! You have just arisen from a long rest and are still rubbing the sleep from your eyes. You are getting up from that old bed and stepping into something new and refreshing to your spirit. Let your mind acknowledge this is what change looks and feels like. Be good to yourself. Give yourself the courage to move through this process. Celebrate change knowing you are simply shedding what is no longer making your heart sing."

Q. How can I be happy with my work?

"We say unto you, follow your bliss! Go out into the world and do whatever work that brings you heart-felt joy and that inspires you to want to repeat the work again the next day. Always ask yourself, "What can I do to accomplish my highest good and have that also affect the highest good of those whose lives I touch? I am ready, open, willing and able to adjust my life according to God's Will."

Listen for the voice within you to answer you.

Develop this inner listening skill where you hear the voice of God's speaking into your heart. Quiet your mind and allow the voice of God to be heard."

Affirmation to Know
My Rightful Career Path

"From the Lord God of My Being, I trust my inner source of Divine Wisdom to lead me in such a way as I will know in my heart my true purpose and worth. I follow that which unfolds to bring me the wealth and happiness I desire and which is given me as my birthright.

Let this be my prayer today and all the days that follow. So be it."

Changes and Breaking Patterns

"The only thing constant is change." -Ralph Waldo Emerson

Meditation for Going Through Changes

"Welcome to the world, this bright and glorious day. Walk with us a while and see as we see. See how beautiful you are. Let us come together and be joyous, for never again shall we see another day quite like this. We bring with us the sun – the Light you seek – and place its radiance in you to shine as a golden star within your heart. It pulsates new life at the very core of your being.

You are like a flower, a bud in the early stages, yielding your petals to the winds of change that blow around you. There is nothing to fear. It is only the stem bending to strengthen itself and make you strong in the face of a challenging wind. Now is the season for you to spring forth in all your radiance. Awake to this moment and live, for happy is your heart to open. Be not afraid to step into life, for the bud becomes a flower. It is time for you to blossom, dear precious one. Let the petals fall to earth's floor, for the bud unfolds to the glory that dwells within it. It is indeed the moment you have waited for."

Q.Why is change so difficult? Why do we resist it so?

"We say that change appears difficult to you because you see only one side of the equation. Change is simply the act of giving up something in exchange for something else. If you do not see what you are getting in return for what you are giving, there is fear attached to the expectation. You judge this based on your past. You associate 'change' with 'pain' instead of for the glory that it could be.

We ask you to contemplate this question: What if you never changed your bath water? The way we see it, any change you face in life should be as clear to you as this question is. Let us give you a new idea to put into your consciousness. *Change is good! Change is prayer in action!*

It is universal energy at work to bring about the desires in your heart that you have asked for. If you resist change, you actually stop the flow of universal energy, and because energy has to manifest somewhere, it will be expressed on your plane as either the lifeblood of answered prayers, or if this natural flow is stopped, it will express as stress in your life, or as illness in the body.

We say this is why disease and health are on the flip side of the same coin. You choose which side you will experience. Have faith, Dear Ones, that *change is only the friction that produces Light.* The Universe is simply responding to your soul's request to graduate to a higher level. You change your bath water, don't you? We suggest that you see all your changes in the same way.

Remember, change simply means you are giving up something you no longer need in exchange for something you want. Therefore, we say *change is good!"*

Q. How can I change my self-sabotaging behavior?

"We see that as soon as you change your self-defeatist attitude to a self-winning attitude, great changes will take place in you. This must first occur on the mental level in your mind's eye. Picture your new self as often as possible, filling in the image with every detail you can imagine, seeing yourself as prosperous, successful and as happy as you dare to dream. Give this new self image as much energy as you did your old self image, and don't give up.

We say that once you accept this new self totally, you

shall see this new self alive on the physical plane. As fast as you are able to turn this thinking around is as fast as you will see your attitude change."

Q. I want to relocate to another state and I wonder if such a move is for my highest good?

"We say, check out the motive behind your desire to move. If it is an escape, we remind you that you cannot run from yourself. If you choose to relocate to a far off place purely out of preference, and you love and approve of yourself, you shall create happiness no matter if you stay or go. You must first realize you create your world wherever you decide to settle.

Check your intentions. Are you running away from or running to something that promises greener pastures? Ask and your heart will tell you. You need not travel far to find your joy. Joy is found within a contented heart."

Q. My husband is retiring from his job soon and I am afraid his being home all the time will disrupt my lifestyle. How can I cope with this upcoming change?

"The answer to your worry is so very simple, that when you see it, it will make you laugh. The human condition has you thinking and believing that your life is so complicated, so complex, that surely your answers must be impossible.

We say unto you, you're at the helm of your own ship. Your future is laid out before you by your own thoughts and reactions to life. You have given much worry to what your life will be like when your husband is around all the time, that if you fear this will be a disaster, you will definitely create some form of personal disaster.

Why not believe in miracles? People can appear to be a certain way, but then, all of a sudden they are quite different than you thought? This response takes place within your own perception. You change your thoughts about someone, and *poof!* they suddenly appear to change.

We suggest a new thought process here. Start visualizing your life as you would really love your life to be instead of imagining what you don't want. Imagine all of the details exactly how you would love it to be. Believe in and trust these new ideas, for they shall create a new outlook in you. See the simplicity here.

Change your perception and it will be as though a magic wand has been waved over you. *Open up and lighten up!* Change is occurring, yes, but change does not mean disaster. Open to receive it and let yourself be blessed. Let yourself be free to new ideas and laughter shall fill you up instead of tears."

Q. Will my children be safe and well during the changes taking place in my life?

"Your children know what is happening to you. They have chosen to be with you throughout all your upcoming changes. They have mastered the art of releasing loved ones and have come into this life to assist you in your letting go. They understand that nothing stays the same. They know change is what is real and constant. They are attuned to the feelings with their hearts and do not have fear about what tomorrow might bring.

We say, *learn from them!* They are with you to teach you how to remain in present consciousness, where you are in complete control over your creative power."

Chronic Fatigue Syndrome

"Vigor is contagious, and whatever makes us either think
or feel strongly adds to our power and enlarges our field of action."
-Ralph Waldo Emerson

Q. I would like to be healed of my chronic fatigue and sore throat. I also want to move away from my parents' house but I cannot seem to budge. What's going on?

"You are experiencing a sore throat for something is trying to be expressed, but you "fight" it. It is lodged in your throat center. You fear others will not support you and your ideas. You have been reluctant to leave home because your parents make it easy for you to stay there. You don't really need to express yourself while you are there, nor take any risks from living in the world-at-large. You don't have to take a risk as long as you are under the safety of your parent's wings.

You have grown more and more discontent with this lifestyle, and would much rather speak up, spread your wings and fly away from the nest. The tiredness is caused from your mentally re-hashing this same question laboriously, over and over again. Change this pattern and you will come alive with new energy and unsurpassed strength.

We say unto you that all disease is caused by thought, and by changing the thought, you change your experience of it. If you do not know exactly what step to take first, there are people who are able to assist you with this. The teachers always appear as soon as you are ready to do the inside work and totally release the need for illness.

Start by changing the thought from needing the problem to a willingness to learn from it. In doing so, the illness is released from you, the lesson learned, and only health and peace of mind takes its place."

Q. What is the cause and how may I heal of Chronic Fatigue Syndrome?

"The manifestation known in your world as chronic fatigue syndrome has manifested in you because you have consistently and persistently allowed yourself to be over-powered by others - on both sides of the veil. These beings willfully take whatever power they can get.

Your healing can begin as soon as you willfully call back your power and keep it. Say the following prayer out loud so we can hear you."

Prayer to Call Back Your Personal Power

"From the Lord God of my being, I declare peace to reign in and throughout my entire being and in my house from this day forward. I release the powerlessness I thought was my reality and call forth the Angels of Light to enter and work with me to accomplish my healing. Let me remember that I am from the Kingdom of Light. I see only Light and goodness wherever I go. I am the radiant Golden Light. My physical surroundings reflect this truth.

I draw my strength from the Great White Light of God and His universe now and forevermore. I have all the energy I need today to accomplish all my goals and I joyfully take dominion over my life and affairs. I know that all I do this day is for my highest good. I look to the outcome I desire. The past no longer has any power to pull me down and tire me out. I let go of all thoughts that obscure my highest intentions, for my will is now in alignment with God's Will. As I lift my eyes up, I draw all good unto me. Nothing in my world can stop me from accomplishing what I am here to do. Amen.

"We say unto you, let these words speak for you now, for they shall give you great new inner strength. Realize the depth of their meaning and say them knowing they bring you the changes you desire to see in yourself and your surroundings, now and forever."

Creating and Manifesting

"The great thing in the world is not where we stand,
but in what direction we are moving." -Oliver Wendall Holmes, Sr.

Q. Why am I on Earth?

"We say, you are on Earth to learn how things feel, how they look, how they sound, how to communicate and how to create. You are co-creators with God. You are here to experiment so you can learn to create what you truly desire.

Now, if you have created something in your life that has not brought you joy, say to yourself, 'Okay, I tried that, I didn't like it, so I don't need to do that again.' Try different things. If it hasn't brought you joy, we say, step back, gather yourself together and choose again.

Try something else! You have spent too much time and energy digging ditches alongside your path rather than traveling onward, down the road."

Q. Will we ever build a larger house than the one we just built?

"From our perspective, we do not understand the concern over spaces called 'largeness' or 'smallness,' or why this is important to the heart. You are given free will on that plane to create your life at your discretion. It is indeed a fact that your thoughts, desires or fears, if given your personal power and attention, will eventually manifest. This is why we caution you to keep watch over your thoughts.

If you truly desire to build yet a larger house, it shall happen. If you put your foot down, so to speak, and decide that you have had enough of building houses, that is what you will create. Take a good look at what it is you hold important in your heart and put your energy on what is the most important. Remember, you are the architect.

We say, watch very closely every thought and every word you speak as if it were to manifest instantly, for on another level this is the truth. It just takes more time on your physical plane for manifestation to occur for you to see it. Then, usually by that time you have forgotten that you gave birth to that thought, and then it is too late, the experience is yours!

We also say unto you that this is like a trial run for you. You see, when you have mastered third dimension, you will "graduate" into the next level of consciousness where your thoughts manifest very quickly.

Take advantage of the reprieve right now and examine your creative thought process. In that next world you have little time to make corrections. We say unto you, learn the process well, here and now."

> "If everything's under control, you're going too slow."
> -Mario Andretti

Q. Should I pursue road racing?

"We say, have fun and love doing whatever you wish to do, or it could be a hollow victory. Choose wisely and follow what is in your heart, for it shall always lead you into joy-filled experiences.

So, now we ask you, what is truly the desire in your heart? Look to that place within you and radiate love into your dreams and aspirations. If you are coming from a goal of, he who dies with the fastest car wins, we say you shall manifest fast cars. We also ask you to contemplate, wins what?We are here to tell you that fast cars is not why you are on the Earth, but it is okay to have fun with whatever brings you joy while you are there.

We say to you, prioritize your goals and know that you

can have all the desires in your heart. Check your intention, and check the motivation behind the things you do.

Remember, regardless of your goal, always extend love in reaching for it, for that will be returned to you and bless your life."

Dependency

"Love does not consist in gazing at each other but in looking outward together in the same direction." -Antoine de Saint-Exupéry

Q. Sreper, what is the lesson for women in attracting unfortunate and unhappy situations in their relationships with men? There seems to be a lot of relationships that are steeped in dependency. Would you shed some light on this?

"There are many, many women walking the Earth these days experiencing the lessons you speak of. In fact, there are more women learning independence, that is, learning to depend on themselves and on their own Spirit, than those who are not. The belief pattern of leaning upon another being started in your Earth near the very beginning, when you perceived the separation as real and found yourselves living in a world of duality, for as soon as you perceived duality; you also realized there were opposites. You then started comparing one to another and therefore saw competition; always seeing one as 'better than another.' Male dominance was the rule and for centuries upon centuries of incarnations in the physical realms, woman acted out the role of being 'the weaker sex.'

Male dominance ruled, both on a personal and Universal level. In fact, humanity isn't seeing both sides as being completely equal yet. Little faith is held in female capabilities and this has not allowed a woman to head your government yet. This dependence issue is a very long-standing, societal belief in inequality, rooted deep in your history and deep within your DNA structure. It is a Universal lesson, hitting home in the hearts of women everywhere.

The larger reality is to know that this is the appointed time in Earth for male/female equality to be fully realized. There is good reason for the seeming 'power struggles' that are in relationships at this time.

Graduation time is upon you, Dear Ones. This lesson will be learned in each and every heart on Earth, one by one, and with the speed-enhancing news media, it won't take the 100th monkey very long to spread this notion of equality near and far. Thereafter, not a single person will be left to suffer in ignorance and inequality any longer.

Now, we see that your knowing this does not make the lesson any easier to do, and we do not imply that it is. But allow us to give you a larger picture of this reality. This lesson was formulated by your Higher Self for you to understand you are not in need of another person, for their approval or anything else. Women have been raised to believe they need a man to care for them because they are considered to be the 'weaker sex' but, Dear Ones, this is not the truth.

We suggest that from this moment forward you re-evaluate how it is you view your life. We suggest you start by re-thinking the way you want your life to be. Do whatever you need to do to accomplish this change in mind, for it is the most important thing for you to do now. There is nothing the matter with you.

Do not judge and punish yourself as though there were something the matter. The notion to lean on another being has served its purpose and all that is left for you to do is release it. It is an evolutionary thing that dependence was a part of your Earth learning, but you have graduated. You need only learn self-love and self-esteem now and realize that you need to go forward without looking back on this. There's nothing to judge, it just is.

We say that by your doing this act of mental releasing, you shall gain a new lease on your life and affairs. All the experiences and the people and the things that were a part of the past learning, the things that brought you to where you are today, were all necessary for this next step to take place. It is very important to bless them all, for without these things you would not be ready to move on.

Go forward now and love and honor yourself like you have never done before. Ask and we will help you do this. All you need do is ask, give us your commitment and we will help you go forward into a new day. The painful situations are only extensions of your reluctance to release what you thought you needed to depend on. Reluctance to release these old thought forms creates resistance to the new relationships and wonderful good that is waiting to come into your life.

Therefore, if you want change, release the hold the past has on you. Meditate and affirm your new convictions of pure Love and Light and Truth to be the path your heart will take today. As much as you can devote yourself to this new practice mentally, the sooner you will realize an independent and happy life springing forth from within you.

Pick up the pieces of yourself that you have scattered about, and bring them home. Bring yourself home. Learn to look inside of yourself for your direction, rather than to seek outside advice – even from your dearest friends, for this is where dependency originates. These caring people, although they may have your best interests at heart, do not walk your path and cannot learn or remove the lessons intended for you to walk through. It is your soul's desire to discover your truth within your own heart; to hear your own inner voice.

We see that a large part of what saddens you is that you have offered your power to others who have gladly taken it and now hold it from you to control you with it. This causes you to get angry and into a cycle of unhealthy attachments. To end this, call upon your own power, bring it home and be whole once again.

You shall be given all the answers you need to experience a full and rewarding life, rich with beautiful, harmonious relationships. You only need to make a decision to let go of what no longer serves you on the highest level. Trust in your angels to guide and help you and relax in your centered self. You are a child of the universe who deserves to have every desire fulfilled, but you must accept it in order to receive it.

Making a decision like choosing the right doctor will become simple and easy to do. Running to someone to seek their advice will only continue to throw you off your center by allowing your power to seep into someone else's answer.

Discover your own power. You are graduating to new heights. This will show up in new friends. The old will always disappear as you graduate and let go of the what no longer serves you. You have the universe at your command, we say allow it to work for you.

Depression

"When you are sad, know this need not be. Depression comes from a sense of being deprived of something you want and do not have. Remember that you are deprived of nothing except by your own decisions, and then decide otherwise." -A Course In Miracles

Q. What is the best way to work through and overcome depression so I may enjoy life?

"We say to you the best way to work through depression, although it is not work at all, is to let go, let go, let go. Know that life is a series of ever-changing events and scenarios. Learn to adapt to this. Let go of your hold onto things that no longer serve your highest purpose. Cancel all thoughts that are not for your highest good. Allow things to move through your life with ease and with grace.

Keep looking forward with expectation of the good you wish to be in your reality. Keep watch over all of your thinking, for it is in this activity of mind that creates the physical reality you see.

Dear Ones, we remind you that you are not powerless on Earth, although mass-consciousness has you locked into this believing in this limitation. Break through that barrier into knowing how unlimited you are, for that will free you. You are the Creator of your experience. If something pulls you down, we suggest that instead of being frightened or depressed over it, embrace the experience. Bless it for bringing you a valuable lesson. Then, when that knowledge is garnered, you have the freedom to release it into nothingness from whence it came.

So, whenever there is something that troubles you or takes you from your peace, we say, "Bless it into oblivion." Bless the people who brought you the lesson, for it was a brave and loving thing they did for you."

We say that with this adjustment in how you view your life, it will lighten the load tremendously, allowing you to see the brighter side, elevating you out of your despair.

Q. What can be done to overcome depression and enjoy life?

"We see that those who are depressed have lost hope. These people come into physical life to find their spiritual self, however, to them life appears to be one struggle after another. Struggle and pain is all they see and this makes them feel like giving up. The person comes into life armed with ambition to learn love.

If a person is very depressed and there is a suicidal tendency, we say that it is a carry-over from another lifetime in which the person did commit suicide. This tendency will continue until he or she has completely forgiven themselves of that. We say unto them, ask for forgiveness and it is done.

The depressed person needs constant encouragement. We encourage you until you begin to feel the roots of change growing strong beneath your feet. We remind you that everything is a lesson planned by your higher self for the experience. Your old belief pattern said, one must endure pain because, 'no pain, no gain.' But now, we say it is graduation time. You no longer need that lesson.

The choice is yours and we suggest you choose to love and pamper yourself. Your struggle is over. As water seeks its own level, your consciousness also seeks its own level. Whatever you have been feeding yourself, and what you have come to believe about yourself is what your outer world has reflected back to you. It is time to seek a higher consciousness, and as you do, your entire world and your outlook upon it changes!

You might be thinking that it's too hard to change, that

you cannot do it, and so we say release the need for struggle. All of your goals, hopes and dreams manifest with ease and joy. If a struggle should occur, ask what it is trying to teach you. Then, listen to our voice within you and hear the answer. You will be able to turn the situation around and learn from it."

Affirmation to Release Depression and Struggle
"Life is easy. I connect and listen to the voice within that urges me on to my highest and best experience of good. I release all other needs from me. So be it."

"If you should forget and lose you way again, know that God's Voice will gently remind you to come back to this joy-filled path immediately. Yes, Dear One, you can re-program yourself to do this with ease and with joy. We say unto you, you are much in doubt of who you really are.

Your ego has made you feel cut-off from God. God is within you. You have come this time upon the Earth to know this Truth. Many times you have followed the noblest path you thought would lead you directly to God outside of you. Your search has been endless and unfruitful, causing your depression. It is time to lift the veil and remember you are a part of God Himself manifested in Creation.

Your profound desire to know God has led you in this journey on Earth. Now, look within. We are not speaking about the God you find in religious books or in your Sunday rituals. God is everywhere. He is within you! He is the air you breathe and the ground upon which you walk. God isn't hidden away somewhere never to be found or known.

Through centuries of guilt and rage, humans have buried themselves, their God-Selves, under the rubble of

Heaven. God never took Heaven away from you. It is in you forever and cannot be diminished, but it can be forgotten. You have been sleeping, and in your sleep you have been dreaming. This is your awakening."

Diet, Food and Eating Patterns

"Watch your thoughts; they become words. Watch your words; they become actions. Watch your actions; they become habits. Watch your habits; they become character. Watch your character; it becomes your destiny." -Unknown

Q. Sreper, how important is it to eat a natural food diet? Does it really matter what we eat?

"We see how out-of-touch human beings have become with the natural cycles of the Earth plane. Man has manipulated the food supply to where it is no longer recognizable by its own kingdom. The farmers have sprayed the crops to death, literally, and have reinvented what has become your edible animals, such as your chickens, as they are genetically unrecognizable to us. Their spirits have been banished. They are raised only to be slaughtered and so the spirit never actually develops into what they were originally created to be.

This is a very sad state to see man manipulate nature for profit and not for the benefit of the people and the planet as a whole. We dare say that it is of the utmost importance to find your way back to living a natural lifestyle according to the natural life cycles on the planet. That would include eating a natural diet.

There is a very good reason for eating seasonal foods and foods that grow naturally in your local vicinity. What you eat is what your body ultimately becomes. We are speaking on many levels here. Find the balance within you to know which foods are best for your particular body type and blood type. Eat a light diet, foods that are filled with Light and of equal importance, we say you need to unceasingly police your thoughts. Scrutinize what your mind is also 'consuming' and become particularly aware of negativity, and then weed those thoughts out. All of these elements blend together to become who you are.

We look back in your history and see a time where your physical bodies were totally sustained by the fruits and grains that abundantly covered the Earth. Foods of that day helped humans sustain youthful health, even if they aged to a thousand years old!

Contemplate what has changed from that time to now. There were no hospitals and no medicine as you know of today, for there was no need for them. The nutrients the body needed were abundant in the foods the people grew in their gardens, hand-picked and ate. Unfortunately, this simple life style is no longer practiced.

Eating healthy is, perhaps more of a challenge today, but it is possible to get back to nature again. You can learn from your ancient manuscripts. Find out how your native peoples of long ago ate and worshiped. Glean this quiet knowledge from them and apply it to your life. A balance must be restored in order for you to be happy and healthy; to be fruitful and multiply.

By the same law, the more imbalance you consume, the further out of balance your life becomes. We wish you to live in peace. May you be open now to dig deep within you, for all truth lies in you... sleeping, perhaps, but ready to be awakened. Be in touch with who you really are and get back into balance with nature."

Q. Sreper, can the human race survive and reproduce well into the future if we continue to poison our foods and our environment as we are now?

"No, it cannot survive if this continues. Poison in, poison out. If you feed yourselves negative or poisonous beliefs, you will develop negative, or poisonous lives filled with disease and suffering. On the other hand, if you feed yourself positive thoughts and positive foods, you will reap positive health and happiness.

We see the human dilemma that you mention in your question and it is with much sadness we see the harm being done to the planet and your food supply. This issue shall face mankind for there has never been any conscious forethought as to what would become of the Earth if manipulation of the food source was allowed to continue. It has been a free-for-all where the ego has been running rampant and forever doing as it pleased without recompense.

There is now a conscious awakening moving over the planet. It will take many human beings to realize what has been happening through this senseless control over the elemental kingdoms. The human ego has gone on with wild abandon, wreaking much havoc on the planet, and it is time to give the power back to Mother Nature, for she will restore Earth to its natural balance and proper frequency. She needs your help to accomplish this. Because there is a co-creative partnership among the kingdoms, your love and awareness is needed to accomplish a balance.

As long as you choose to cloak yourselves in physical armor (a body), and for as long as you reside in physical reality, you shall need Mother Earth to be your stage on which to carry yourselves. (And assuming this is the case, we are answering your question in those terms)."

Glory of Light Meditation
"In meditation, hold Mother Earth in the Glory of God's Holy Light. Direct your Love and Light into her very core which then emanates and pulsates outward into the universe. See this Light flowing and spiraling throughout her inner core, expanding

outward, completely penetrating the Mineral Kingdom, through the rocks, faults and fissures, mending them all.

Then, see this healing Light traveling throughout the entire Plant Kingdom, filling the trees, plants, flowers and crops with its glowing Light, pulsating further into all the physical elements of Earth, through the air and through the waters, until every element in every kingdom is restored to its original vibrancy intended by the Creator.

And so it is."

"Mother Earth has been tolerant of the abuse. She has carried a heavy burden far too long and she cannot carry it any further. You hold the key with your love. As you begin to let the darkness go out of your individual lives, you shall also lighten her load, for she carries you. She carries all of you, without judgment, and has always accepted what has been given her without question or complaint.

But the negativity from the ego simply cannot go on any longer. The thought-form of hatred is dark and dreary, and carries the the heavy message of fear. Life on Earth has always been about the ego satisfying itself at another's expense and this will no longer be tolerated. This is the dawn of a new day. The Light has come. The dark age shall be put to rest but cannot retreat until each and everyone of you who reside on Earth decides to live in Light.

Become aware of all that you can to help make the world a Garden of Eden again. Stop manipulation of the lower kingdoms, for what has happened was not what the Creator meant by giving man dominion over them. The plants and the animals are your brothers and sisters. They need your love and honor just as you also need what they offer you. The poisoning of man must stop as the toxic sprays on crops must stop. Man's negative belief systems must stop as the genetic manipulations must stop. Man's sleeping consciousness is poisonous to the human mental body, just as the actual contaminants being placed on your food supply are poisonous.

Let go of your interest in these dark matters. Turn toward the Light and allow nothing less than Light to enter into your mind or into your life again. If this seems like an impossible task to overcome, we shall tell you that with your choosing to live in Light and Love and join with your Father/Mother God to help raise Earth into her next stage of evolution, this shall be the easiest task ever accomplished, for it shall be done with the power and support of all the Universe itself.

Join with us today. The Light calls you home. Let the world of the Angels of the Great White Light wash over you as a fresh Spring rain prepares the Earth for receiving new seeds. Allow a new reality to emerge, just as you would expect to have a panoramic garden spring up from planting the finest flower bulbs.

When working with the land, always do it with love and appreciation. Talk to the grass, the trees, the shrubs. Give them your love. Tell them your intentions. Listen to theirs. Treat them as you would your dearest, supporting friend, for this is not far from the truth. They hear you and they rejoice knowing you are connecting with them.

Call on the devas to direct your intentions in your garden. Call on the diva of the grass before you mow your lawns. Call on the devas of the trees before pruning or cutting unwanted growth. Work with nature in partnership. Allow yourselves to be amused at this re-connection and you will be amazed at harvest time. What you give forth now shall be returned a thousand times then, so be careful as to what seeds you are truly planting.

Garden with love. Thank the plant kingdom for its abundance, its love and its energy. What you feed it, feeds you. Prepare your foods with love and put that vibration into you as you eat from your garden. Then replace the energy you take by nurturing the soil for planting again next season. We say unto you that thoughtless manipulation cannot be tolerated any longer. It is why there is so much dreaded dis-ease on the planet. Your precious bodies cannot take the influx of poisons, in any form any longer.

Nature begs you to stop all unloving practices and begin again. What ever you put forth in any effort, gardening or other work, remember that it is the energy of that intention that multiplies and returns to you. Choose wisely dear ones, and live healthy and happy lives on Mother Earth, for when you do, she responds in kind."

Q. What is the reason I put on extra weight?

"We say you had chosen to put on extra weight to protect yourself from what you perceived to be a cruel world. You are afraid to really let anyone come in close enough to you, for you fear you will lose a part of yourself. This is not so, and your own soul knows this, but the time to love is now. You do not have to become something more than you already are. Allow yourself to get to know the real you underneath the covering called excess weight. Do not be afraid to uncover your truth. It shall be symbolic of shedding the old skin to reveal the beauty underneath.

When was the last time you gave yourself permission to accept yourself the way you are, and to love yourself for who you are right now? Your soul has chosen this path for a very good reason. You have been afraid of yourself, your own powerful self. It seems you chose to crawl under a rock and hide, not believing you could come out and have fun on Earth. We say there is nothing for you to cover up anymore, you only thought there was. Release the need to cover up anything anymore and be who you are.

If you feel fearful of what we say, go within and ask yourself what you are afraid of. The weight shall disappear as the need for added protection is released. As you go within and uncover your real self, do not be afraid of what is in there. You need no protection from Love. Drop your fear and drop the weight. With an open and receptive mind say the following prayer:

A Prayer for Ideal Weight

"God, I ask to be released from the idea that I am separate from you. That has somehow led me away from my knowing the truth of who I am. I ask to be re-united with you in total Oneness now.

I have previously forgotten that you have given me a choice and I now choose to see the Light in me, and in everyone I meet. I am no longer afraid to reveal to the world my divinity. I now manifest exactly who I am. I ask that any and all barriers I have made to protect myself from the love I feared, be removed completely, leaving me free to love myself as I am, and as I wish to be.

I allow myself to be joyous within your creation, and I release the need for any protection I thought I needed. I go forward now in confidence knowing that I am my perfect weight. The more I release my fears, the more I love. And the more I love, the less I need the protection of extra body weight! I give thanks that this is so. Amen."

Q. Why did I gain weight?

"In the True Essence of Who you are, Dear Child of God, you are Light. You are not your physical body, however, your physical body will always reflect to you what you believe about yourself. We suggest you stop fighting the weight gain and transform that energy into loving and nurturing yourself instead.

Drop the resistance and you drop the excess weight. Love and embrace who you are *right now.* Love and accept yourself no matter how much you weigh. As you allow your Light to shine forth, one of two things will happen; you will either no longer be concerned with how much you weigh, or the added weight will simply melt away. Remember, your true self is Light and Light has no weight."

Q. What can I do to lose weight quickly and keep it off forever? Also, what can I do to stop being so obsessed about this?

"We see you have spent your mental energy on the struggle of weight gain, rather than with the solution. Whatever you give your attention or power to will manifest. Fears manifest as easily as dreams. The universe is indifferent to your wishes.

To overcome this obsession, allow yourself to think only of the results you want to see. Give no more mental energy to that which you do not want. Stop yourself in midthought if you have to. Stop thinking obsessively, and you will stop acting obsessively.

Do not be hard on yourself if you falter at first, but rather be good to yourself as you would be to a newborn baby. You would not scold the baby for not knowing something he is too young to know. We see you as a newborn baby, new to this idea of creating a new body.

Treat yourself well. Love yourself dearly. If you slip backwards, simply notice that you slipped. Pick yourself up, put your mind back on your goal, and try again."

Disabilities

"Men are disturbed not by things,
but by the view which they take of them." -Unknown

Q. We do a lot of healing work at my church which also provides handicapped parking spaces. My opinion is, let's heal these people and they won't need special parking spaces, wheelchair ramps, etc. Can you please comment?

"The people to whom you refer, the ones you have judged to have these so-called disabilities, have selected their particular set of circumstances, just as you have also selected yours. The difference is their physical handicaps are visible to the naked eye, and yours may not be so noticeable. We would like to interrupt this line of thinking/judging you have. Wouldn't it be wonderful, once and for all time, to stop such judging? Man has too long been in the habit of looking upon the ones who walk with difficulty as though there is something the matter with them that must be fixed. We say, that those you judge as having physical handicaps do not look upon you and wonder what is the matter with you!

Dear Children of God, you are all children of the same God. You must remember that you have all come into Earth school to learn various aspects about yourselves, about your creation and to find God within you. Each of you has selected the conditions in which you will best learn these various things. Now, we further remind you that it was the One you refer to as the Christ who came upon your dark star some 2,000 years ago with but one message for you to follow. He said to love one another and do not judge, for you cannot see where you are and cannot see who walks beside you on your path.

You have heard the saying that unless you have walked

67

in your brother's shoes, judge him not, for you do not know where he has been or where he is going. This is the truth and we say abide in it. Unless you release your concern over what your neighbor is creating as his reality, you can never be at peace with your own internship - which is the real reason you are on the Earth.

Indeed, it is a noble thought to wish everyone be healed. It is our own desire and purpose to see all of Creation's children walking in the Light, bright and shining once more. We can only wait until their minds are ready to accept this Light and Love of God fully into their hearts.

We are on hand to send this healing when asked. We join with you in your prayers, for it is through these words and thoughts that the heavy veils can finally be lifted, allowing the Light of Heaven to shine brilliantly in. Our purpose is to hold that thought, even when humanity has forgotten this truth. We always welcome you to join with us. In the months and years to come, the energy of the world shall be changing. Even though it seems humanity moves ever so close to the edge of night, this Light shall prevail, and all will receive a healing in their hearts and minds.

We await that glorious day with great anticipation, for indeed, all shall witness when Heaven engulfs Earth and lifts Her up into the pristine Radiance of God, and we are all home once again."

Divorce

"It is in letting go what you think is real
that you gain what is eternal." -Sreper

*Q. Divorce is really scary. How can I understand all of
the mixed emotions I have regarding my divorce?*

"Trust that whatever occurs between you and your ex-
spouse happens as a gift to you. Certain things come before
you on your life's path for you from which to grow and
learn. To be at peace with this process we suggest you send
Pure Love into your ex-spouse's heart, and not judge them
in any way. Remember, that what you send out in thought
creates what you will experience. Judge not and you are not
judged.

Treat your ex-spouse in the manner you wish to be treated. You are simply on a journey and you are just moving
through this valley, not building your home there. Remove
the circumstances that have caused you pain out of the context in which you are viewing them and place them in the
Pure Consciousness of Love.

Your ex-spouse also has a curriculum. We suggest you
bless your ex-spouse by sending all the Love and Light
from your heart directly into his or her heart without further
ado. Hatred never healed a thing. Love heals all. Let this
Love/Light wash over both of you like a shower flowing
directly from God. This is simply your lesson in forgiveness. You see, it is in letting go what you think is real that
you gain what is eternal."

Q. How can I get through my divorce peacefully?

"We say, choose to see peace and release the notion of
anger and spiteful revenge. Bless your departing partner
now. See them wrapped in the warmth of God's Love and

divinely perfect where they are. See them as being warm and friendly to you throughout the divorce procedure. No matter how bitter this battle had been, it can be turned around. The illusion is the anger manifested, but illusions change. Bless your ex-spouse and release him or her. In doing this, you release yourself. Extend the love that abides in you and love is what shall manifest in your outer world and throughout all your relationships."

Q. Please help me. I am afraid I will lose out in my settlement. How can I stop worrying over this?

"We say, you cannot lose out. You have everything to gain. Give your ex-spouse what they want and stand tall doing it. What you gain will far exceed the material goods that can be replaced. Take only what is yours and leave the rest. You know in your heart what those things are. Do not be vindictive, but bless and release. Call on your angels. Ask us to guide you and we are there to assist you always. You do not go through this alone.

We say, humans, put extreme amounts of energy and worry into the money you have and the money you do not have. We suggest you remember you are a child of a generous and loving Father. You are Creation in its Glory, yet you hardly react to these words when we say them. Your glorious self remains intact as God created you. You have been given the gift to co-create with God and we say you are constantly creating the world you walk in. You forget this in your physical disguise, the camouflage which shrouds you in forgetfulness.

Remember, you can re-create what you have. There is abundance and wealth in your world beyond your wildest dreams. You need only to call forth what is divinely yours and it will come to you. Seek what is yours by birthright and be careful not to call for anything that is not yours. The following prayer may benefit you."

Prayer for Divine Settlement

"Create in me a new spirit, O God, and lead me to knowing there is plenty for each and everyone of your children, regardless of what I see. Teach me that what is mine comes to me exactly when it's needed. I am well and I am wealth! I am provided with what I need now and always. I remove my fears and my fences which limit my divine settlement. I open myself to receive God's direction, knowing in my heart the way of my good is open to me now. Amen."

Q. I deeply love my ex-wife and cannot move on since our divorce. Help!

"You shall always be disappointed if your back is against the Light. It is as though you are standing in the doorway to a new kingdom, but you are facing it backwards. You are fixed on what has happened and not on what can be. Remember, the world is in a constant state of flux and wherever you place your values, that is what will appear to have value to you.

What is needed now is for you to see another way of looking at this, for once you have new enlightenment you cannot return to the old consciousness. You are feeling sad because you do not yet see the possibilities ahead for you. We see you have lost yourself in her. You have relied on her to bring you the happiness and fulfillment you desire from this lifetime, but we say that is quite a load to place on another person. You are the only one who can bring happiness to you."

Q. If I go through with my divorce, where would be a good place for me to start over?

"The physical location does not matter to us. That is seen as merely a choice you make based on your personal preferences. What we say unto you is look into your heart, for this is where you start over.

We see that you are really jumping way ahead of yourself and wanting to make very quick decisions. Stay in the moment. Period. You do not need to make decisions before it is time to make them, for that only causes you stress and worry. We say, ease up on yourself. Throw your watch away and learn to live from your heart, from that life force so strong within you, that loves you so much, it would never give you a wrong move. Listen to it. Start over by following your heart, not your head.

You have so much to give to your world and so much to gain. It all lies waiting for you to say "yes" to it. Clear away the cobwebs of the past and forgive the should-have-beens. Let it all go. Let only love fill your mind and heart, and it will tell you your next step. Until then, smile, and remember you are loved beyond the words we have written here."

Q. I am facing a divorce from my wife who is filled with anger. What is the lesson in this situation, and how can I release what is happening?

"Dear One, you cannot control another person, but you can extend more Love to them. Be kind to her in thought, word and deed no matter what her reaction to you is. This may be difficult to do at times, but the rewards will be great. All disputes shall disappear into the bright Light of forgiveness, and Love will prevail. The greatest miracle seen on Earth is one where an ancient hatred melts in Love's warm embrace. Keep looking up and see your own miracle here.

Here is a prayer to stay focused on Love working out its plan in you and her. To see love, be loving!"

Prayer To Return To Love

"I ask that Love prevail in me and in my life now and from this moment forward through time. I release from me all past judgments I have made against me, against Love, and against all others in my life. I accept the Love and Life of God into myself right now. I radiate the strength this Love gives me to all people and it is accepted and returned to me. I find my way in this life, and I am happy now. I ask that I be led in ways that lead me to my highest good, releasing all things that make me unhappy. I release myself from judging others knowing that the Love of God surrounds and protects me always. Only goodness and kindness can be the results I see. I am grateful knowing Love prevails in my life. Amen."

"Return to Love, Dear Ones in Earth, the days are much too short to continue life in darkness and rage. Love yourselves now and reach out in love to those who are crying for it. Turn on the Light and walk out of night into day.

The time is now for this to be put behind you. Great are the rewards that lie ahead. We want you to be there to receive them."

Q. How can I best help my children through our divorce?

"Changes bring forth bright new beginnings and we see you are being prepared for them. Your children know what is happening too, and although they do not like to see their parents separate, they are with you to also experience this path of the heart. They chose to be in a place where love would endure, even through the seeming 'loss' of a parent.

Your children are present for this to provide you with their love and assuredness so you may see the Light and be at peace. Always be up front and honest with your children. Never lie to them. They know or sense things and they love you regardless. Be honest and gentle. Remember, you cannot make a mistake, but you can make new choices.

Instead of seeing divorce as an ending, we suggest you see it as a new beginning. Thus, it creates a much more positive flow of energy from you to your children, and it will lessen the pain of the experience."

Donating Organs

"The person who walks on the road with an open hand
receives many blessings." -Old Chinese Proverb

*Q. Sreper, on a TV talk show, a woman spoke about the
death of her daughter, as well as the decision to donate her
daughter's organs. Later, the recipient of her daughter's
heart was able to describe the girl's death in detail. Do
organ recipients receive the memories of their donor, and do
you think organ donating is a good and honorable practice?*

"We say unto you that those who believe they are their
physical body are in for a great awakening. Through his
closed-mindedness, man creates a dire need to replace his
broken body parts so he can prolong his fear-filled life on
the physical plane. But that isn't the point. It is sad for us to
see that physical bodies have become marketed as some sort
of commodity. Even the highest bidder has been seen to win
the needed body part. Sad we are, indeed, to see the human
Earth-life focus so misdirected as this.

We use some strong words here, but it is to make a
point. You are not your physical bodies, and you would be
a much happier race of people if you could accept this fact.
Nor are you your ego which is in total alliance with the
physical body. To the ego it would be certain death if you
were to 'jump town' to a higher realm and let go of the ego's
grasp on you. But you must do this to ultimately 'save'
yourselves.

You see, Dear Ones, you have been misled by the ego.
God would not create you and let you live in fear's nasty
grip, only to face total annihilation and abolishment. You
have plodded along the ego's path as an underdog in darkness, fearing your very own shadow long enough. We dare
say that your mission is much more noble than what you

have fallen for and to which you have agreed.

You are on the Earth to release the shadows, not play with them. As children of the Light, you may begin again at any time. If you must insist on giving away your power, give it to your highest self who knows which road will lead you out of hell and into Heaven. We mean this literally.

Be afraid no longer, for you can choose Love instead. It is really very simple, but you see, you've been focused on only the dark and fearful things in life and you haven't seen the Light of day. Perhaps you haven't heard the call going out to you, that in order to change your life, you need only change your mind and choose again. We offer you peace. Turn and face the Light, the Love and the Hope of God. Renew yourselves as children of a bright and glorious Kingdom who are visiting Earth and are there to create only joy for yourselves and others. Make this your one and only goal. Thus far, you have all failed the test, so to speak, and now is a wonderful time to begin again. Forgive yourselves. Get back in control and take a new and higher road.

Everything is energy, and energy is everything. If there are certain thought-forms around a particular organ (also energy), and if the recipient of that organ is sensitive to the subtle worlds of thought, yes, he or she will be able to pick-up messages from that organ.

Some may be very surprising messages too, such as the recollection of the donor's death, or other trauma as it relates to that organ. Some people might even take on any remaining karma of the person who has passed but it is important for you to remember that there are no accidents, only agreements in the Grand Plan.

You have free will on the Earth plane and no one can interfere with what God has set in motion. There are never any accidents, which we hope you have memorized into consciousness now. Those who give and those who receive certain organs have been mapped out by what you refer to as the higher realms of Karma. Remember, no one is to stand in judgment of another's life path or whether or not he donates or receives another's organ.

We, too, are careful not to judge in giving our answer here, as it is terribly wrong to judge those who are not in agreement with what you choose. The act of organ exchange should forever remain an individual choice, and that if each and every person would decide to contact their heart and hear their own inner voice, they would always make the right choice."

Earthbound Spirits

Q. There are several bothersome spirits in and around my house. What do they want and what will make them leave?

"We say you have been giving away pieces of your powerful self, and these earthbound spirits have gladly taken them. There are many souls who feel they are lost on the other side of the veil, but they do not know they are lost. They will draw others' light unto themselves, for they do not know they can turn up their own Light. They have attached themselves to you, for you have allowed yourself to be open to them and 'unprotected.'

Do not be too alarmed for this happened for a good reason on your spiritual path. It is time that they be released to their own path, and you are a helper in this now. We cannot reach them from here because they are too turned away from us and are vehemently focused on the physical Earth.

We must have you totally release them, for this is your release. We say unto you, be stern and persistent and say to them,*"I am not what you seek. Look for the brightest Light that shines and move toward it now. Go to the Light."*

We see that you have been somewhat reluctant to do this releasing for, in a way, you have enjoyed their company. This has given you some excitement, but let them go now and the much greater excitement of peace and tranquility shall take its place. After you release them, you will have a greater sense of power and a lot more energy. You will be able to call your angels and spirit guides with whom you want to communicate. Create healthy relationships, rather than the draining interaction you are now experiencing.

We urge you to not interact with the spirit energies that

are not of the Light of God. Use the following prayer whenever there is an attached entity drawing your power from you."

A Prayer for Freeing Earthbound Spirits

"Dear God, I ask that you usher me to the Light where only You abide and where I see the blessings You have given me. As I am lifted up, I draw only good unto me. I honor all beings who have shared my entity with me, and now I give them permission to go to their highest level of awareness where they are unable to return to me. I bless them and release them now. I denounce all entities that have come into my auric field and I am free. I cast out all demons in thought, word, or deed. I give these souls to you, Dear God, to heal and make whole. Take them where they need to be, and in my releasing them, I am free to walk in the Light where You would have me be. I take command over my body now.

From the Lord God of my being, I command anything that is not here in Love and Light to leave this plane now. So be it. Amen."

Earth Changes

"The laws of chaos govern all illusion." -A Course In Miracles

Q. Sreper, what is the importance of the drama that's unfolding on planet Earth now?

"Dear Ones, we have been waiting forever for this Dawn of Light to come to Earth. It has been so long that, indeed, humanity has nearly forgotten this is what was asked. We are here to say that the Light has arrived and the Earth shall no longer be cloaked in robes of darkness. The unfoldment shall be known far and wide, throughout the heavens as a celebration the likes of which have never been seen. The shimmering sparkle shining brilliantly throughout the nighttime sky will also be reflected in the eyes and souls of the newly awakened. You shall gasp with joy at the sight!

The importance of this great event of Earth's emergence into Light seems so much more powerful because of human anticipation. Be still, for the sights coming upon you at this time shall not be disappointing, the Light of which will be enough to revel in forever.

We say each and everyone of you shall, on some level, experience a storm of sorts, a shakedown of your values and your beliefs. The dramas that you have been creating, and in which you act, shall seem to come upon you as a great wind and wave, loosening the ego's grip on your mind.

But fear not, there shall be smooth sailing following the storm. This shakedown period is necessary for you to be able to further shed any lingering shadows and emerge fully into the Light.

For some people this will seem scary. These folks have preferred to bury their heads in the sand and be oblivious to what is happening "off-shore." Some people have rendered our words of warning to you on the Earth plane as "hearsay," and would choose to go about their tiny, third dimensional world unaffected by the changes that are taking place all around them.

And so, it is to them we say, "Wake up! It is time for you to prepare for the Light to come forth as it has never been before. Arise from your beds of denial and take up your cross and follow Me."

The cross represents your troubles, your burdens and your karma. Pick them all up, and as you do, they shall dissolve into Light leaving your hearts washed and renewed. Our analogy of this time on Earth is that of a washing machine reaching the end of the agitating cycle. You, Dear Ones, are likewise emptying the wash water (karma). You are about to rinse the dirty suds and then go into a spin. When this cycle is completed and you're hanging out to dry, your hearts will know why you needed to go through the process you just completed. The karmic wash, indeed.

Let not your hearts or minds be troubled but hear these words we give to you. What is being (or has been) extracted in this season of washing/cleansing is not needed by your soul in its journey forward. Let go of the old now and forever. You find yourselves in emotional trouble when you look back on what was and on how it used to be, and hold on to it.

See the dawn of Light this new and beautiful day. Realize that the bumpy, stormy ride is about to end for it is graduation time. For some of you it has already ended, and so look ahead to peace, fresh clean peace, undaunted by any darkness lurking any longer. Wipe the sleep from your eyes and hold only thoughts of peace in your mind.

Take this learning a second at a time, and if opposing thoughts arise, gently move your mind back to peace once again, and hold it there. Practice as though your life depended on it, for in a sense it does. Although you may not recognize them, you will see opportunities come to you to learn peace. Remember, these are lessons designed by spirit for your learning."

Q. What can I do about my fears regarding Earth changes and widespread destruction?

"We see the heaviness in your heart that is brought on by your fears and worries over things that we would consider "hearsay." Your mind hasn't developed its ability to use discernment in its study of world events, even those smaller things that happen in your day-to-day life tend to stir a deep reaction in you.

It is your task in this lifetime to uproot out dated and fearful thought forms from within you, for we see that in too many lifetimes you have fallen to others' beliefs and only because you believed them to be true, they became real. You need to be free from this Karma now. What we are about to say to you will take some time and effort on your part to manifest the changes you so desire.

We ask that you give us your willingness and then call upon the elemental kingdom in your prayers daily and ask to be shown what it is you need to know this day. The elementals will respond by filling your heart with love, with a bubbling effervescent light in pink, white and pale blue. Ask your angels to lift your heart from the past into this new presence, for your body can no longer bear the pain of darkness and negativity thrust upon you from the past. Ask to be cleansed and healed of all old dreams you have held deep within you. Ask to be returned to the Light of Wisdom.

We ask that you be shown the way to overcome all these fears, one by one. As you are led to each new freedom, bless the fear, for its journey has brought you to a new gateway.

There wasn't another path for you to take. The fears have served their purpose but are no longer needed. We say, bless them away! Turn your eyes to the heavens and see the blue skies above you, now and forever. In your hearts there is peace, calm and tranquility which shall be your only experience now, if you so choose.

If you should wander again and see something that is fearful, let it go and say, 'These things may happen in the world, but they do not happen in my world.'

Give it no more thought than that, for whatever your mind dwells upon, it creates. Therefore, think only on the things that align with the desires in your heart. We say that within twenty-one Earth days, your heart shall have its wings and fly to new heights. Be diligent about this and keep your eyes on the prize of peace. Let not the outside world disturb it."

Q. I hear many say that great Earth changes are on the horizon and that California may fall into the ocean. I have also heard that I will be told by my guardian angels if I should move to safety. What should I believe? Should I fear these changes?

"We say unto you that if you choose peace, you will see only peace. The Earth plane is a place that supports all creation, on all levels. All thought creates equally regardless if it is constructive or destructive in outcome. That is why your Guardian Angels are making themselves known to you now. You need our guidance to get you out of the mischief you have created. You have been like unruly little children out on the playground without any supervision. You have no idea how powerful you are, and you have been addicted to a negative mind set since "the Fall" of Man into third density. You are beginning to awaken. You are scratching your head and looking around you, wondering what happened.

We say to you, do not fear these changes, for fear drew you into this predicament in the first place. Try love this time. Let loose any idea that comes to you that isn't based in Love, and release them into nothingness. Instead of fear, send your love to the world and see wonderful 'Earth changes' take place!"

Q. I am moving to the East coast which is supposed to sink into the ocean according to some sources. Am I crazy for moving there?

"Rumors have a funny way of spreading. Those who live on the West coast hear that it is California is prophesied to sink into the sea! Do you believe that beauty comes with a price? Does this mean that to live with the beauty of the ocean you must also live in fear of perishing into it?

We say look deeply into your personal beliefs for it is within them you shall have your key. If you lived in the desert and believed you were going to sink into the sea, it would happen unto you just as you believe. You see, it is you who creates your world by your thoughts and beliefs.

We will not take any credit for the power of your own thought and we will not predict any such Earth changes for your vicinity because it is up to your collective-consciousness what happens to you as beings on that plane. We cannot take your creative power away from you.

Be clear about your personal ambitions and intend only to create the good and beautiful, and leave the dark, destructive toys or thoughts alone. The choice is yours to make and we say, make it one that you would like to experience."

Q. I have been preparing for the Earth changes for a decade now. When will they happen?

"You have been following a dream that needed an overhaul for some time. Release the old dream realizing it has been accomplished. Preparation has been your motivation, now we say prepare for what comes next. Expect the unexpected! Follow your bliss! Do not waste your time waiting for Earth changes that may never happen. Set a new goal. Be creative and listen to your inner voice that is lovingly guiding you.

There is much more for you to do so we say get busy. Let limitlessness become your new guiding light. Turn yourselves around and see the Light there beside you. Let your minds be turned around too, and see another world.

Arise and walk in this new Light and find your way home. Blessings shall follow you all the days of your lives. Be kind to yourselves and others, for those that hear these words and follow them shall not perish."

Q. The upcoming Earth changes, quite frankly, spook me. I heard that the water supply will be tainted, food will lose it's life force, not to mention the United States losing much of it's land mass. Where do I stand within this probable situation?

"We say unto you that you create your reality with your thoughts and subsequent belief system. We say that if you truly believe that you will be overcome in a flood, you will be because you have accepted it as a reality for you to experience.

But, we remind you that while the so-called Earth changes seem to loom and threaten, have faith in your Creator. Call upon your higher wisdom and see God as He is. Do not create less than what He would give you. Even though someone else may create disaster in the world, it need not be in your world unless you take it on. It is true that

God gave you power to create as you wish. We say choose wisely what you will have in your experience.

Dear Ones of Light, forget not the journey you embarked upon long ago. We say unto you, welcome to the Earth anew. This is the beginning of the end of darkness. We are very close to the finish line where we shall all throw our hands in the air in celebration of 'mission accomplished,' Light is shining radiantly on the Earth.

Learn peace and patience. Learn to be still in heart and mind and your cups shall be filled and overflowing and you will thirst no more. Embrace yourselves and pat yourselves on the back. You have journeyed far and now it's time to rest awhile. There is still a greater scenario at work. While the rush appears to be on for souls to "graduate" from Earth school, all people are being brought out of fear and darkness and into the Light. This is the cleansing tide of the Earth.

Great changes are upon you now. All secrets are being exposed. Everything is coming into the Light of day. This is just a brief outline of what is happening on your Earth. You may choose to cleanse with love, and know you are safe. Or, you may choose to see these changes as fearful and feel safe nowhere.

We invite you to join with us in the Light. Revel in the peace of God and leave your fears behind. To some, this appears fearful, but that is all that is being accomplished by the so-called, 'Earth changes.'"

Ego

"We don't see things as they are,
we see things as we are." - Anais Nin

Q. Sreper, please tell us about the ego and the truth about making mistakes? It appears the ego can wreak so much havoc!

"We say the ego is, indeed, the 'little self,' but depending on how much power you give it, it may not be so little! Your ego mind will always make you believe you are not worthy of anything better than what it says you deserve. Your first step is to release this judgment.

The ego's path leads you nowhere. You only thought it did. Stop focusing on your ego self and begin to trust your higher self. You are Children of Light and you deserve much, much more than the ego offers you. Whenever your ego stands in the way of you receiving what God gives you, say to it, 'Get thee behind me.' We invite you to join with your Higher Self and release the ego now.

Release the notion that you've made a mistake because in truth, you never have, nor could you. Everything you have experienced has taken place for your education. You haven't 'goofed.' Be ready to move to higher ground, as it were, and into new adventures. You need never repeat the past. Live in the newness that is today and leave the ego in yesterday."

Q. Many times I compare myself to others and it never makes me happy. How can I stop this behavior?

"We say, to stop this behavior, clear your heart of its unwarranted ego longings for what could be and accept what is. Keep yourself open and clear for you cannot see the good in the light of the situation if you keep yourself in the dark. There are many things for you to enjoy and we see that you will be happiest by testing the waters of them all, one by one. And when you're not in the moment of dipping your toes in the water, we see you will enjoy fence sitting.

What we are really saying to you is that wherever you are in your life, it is wise to savor the moment and be content in it, for if you aren't happy, you cannot create happiness by leaping the fence and escaping the yard. For when you are in that other yard looking back over the fence, your own grass will appear greener and you may long after it! Ah, the fickleness of the human ego.

Contemplate these things and relax your ego craziness. See what is really real, enjoy the present moment and let the rest go. Know that it could be that you have been 'saved' of stepping into some disaster, that your feet could have landed on some slippery rocks beneath the surface. Take the fence instead! The wait is never for very long.

So, we say keep yourself clear and tell your heart all is in perfect, divine timing."

Prayer to Align My will with God's Will
"Dear God, I ask that you operate in all the things I encounter today, and that everything I do honors you and honors me. Let me know I am following the path leading me to my ultimate highest good, and to the highest good of those whose lives I touch. Open my ears to hear your Guidance in all my undertakings. I choose to live a joyful and abundant life. I choose to make all my relationships happy and beneficial to me and to those who I associate with. I ask God's Will be done now and always. So be it. Amen."

Elemental Kingdom

"White coral bells upon a slender stalk, Lilies-of-the-Valley deck my garden walk. Oh don't you wish that you could hear them ring? That will happen only when the fairies sing." - Traditional Song

Q. Please describe the elemental kingdoms for us?

"We say, the elemental kingdom is a parallel world to yours. The two are similar but the elemental kingdom has a higher vibration than your physical plane and that is why you normally cannot see the inhabitants there. Both worlds were created at the same time, during what we term 'the Fall from Grace. 'The elementals' purpose was to remember the Oneness for you when you forgot your connection to Source. They are in agreement with the Great White Light to assist those who remain in the dark.

The elementals walk with you on your path. They have always been there and will remain with you until there is no trace of darkness left casting shadows on the world. They are your pals, if you will, and they wish to join with you. They want you to remember them and play and interact with them. They want to help you create joy and happiness in your spirit, and health in your bodies. You could say they are like co-guardians with you, standing guard while you've been away.

With this joyful news we also caution you. It's been a very long time for these beings and they are afraid. Their hearts and their purpose for being on Earth have been heavily trampled upon for centuries. Much human work will be needed to bring back this long-forgotten connection you once had and enjoyed with them. Indeed, some of this work has been happening on your planet already.

After your intention of co-creating with them again is made clear, they will cherish your renewed friendship and will make themselves joyfully known to you once again. We say that this will take some work on your part, but once the bridge is mended, it will be heavily traveled."

Q. How can we work with the elementals?

"The elementals will work with those who are pure in heart and clear in their intention to co-create with them in harmony. They know who you are. You will not be able to fool Mother Nature. Those who delight in working closely with them will be invited to do so. These people will hear the calling and will respond by inviting the spirit of nature into their hearts to also work with them. They will receive instructions intuitively. Those who are trained to hear these messages, will do so.

The devas and nature spirits wish to connect with all the people who work with the land, such as the farmers, the gardeners, the window-sill herbalists, and anyone who has a heartfelt wish to co-create with them. They are excited to be called upon, for their sleep has been sound for a very long time as you know time, and we say they shall respond to your call, for that is what they wait for! In working together with them, use patience and love, for they are yet bashful and a bit mistrusting of human ways.

And do you blame them? They have been put aside and rendered useless when man decided to let his ego run rampant, and began to manipulate the Earth and the crops with his machinery and chemicals, completely disregarding the will of the elemental kingdom and its divine service. We say, however, that once the connection has been re-established, look forward to having fun with them!

Call upon 'the wee folk' whenever your intention is to be outdoors in nature and to heal the Earth, whether it is to plant a garden, to pick a flower, to cut the grass, to prune a tree, to move a rock or stone, to dig a hole, to build a house. We say call on them for permission and for any instructions. You will be amazed at the results which will far exceed your wildest dreams come harvest time."

Q. What is happening in the elemental kingdoms at this time of great change on the planet?

"'The little ones,' as we choose to call them, have long awaited the re-connection with their brothers in human form for they are not the ones who have lost the partnership. They have consistently upheld their promise and their duties to maintain the natural world for everyone. We see the little ones are very busy. They never rest. Humans have long rested and have not kept up their co-creative efforts, thus making the job in the elemental kingdom, long and arduous.

But, we announce that the Light is now shining upon you and no one shall toil as they did before the Light dawned. The result of the Light coming has assisted the little ones in re-connecting with their brothers. We say, some are rejoicing, yet some are cautious due to the long silence between the kingdoms. Theirs is the mirror image of your world. Some folks are awake and filled with Light, while others are not quite ready to fully trust in bright outcomes."

Q. What would better assist me in opening and communicating with the devas, the elementals, and the nature spirits?

"We say to empty your mind of all previous expectations of how you should or should not communicate with this kingdom of beings, releasing all prior knowledge you have accumulated, for none of it will fit in the framework of what is to come when you join with the little ones. The first level of training being presented at this time is for you to practice quieting your conscious mind of all its pre-conceived thoughts.

Elias, the Little One adds, 'Feed it freedom and then, feed it more freedom. Expand all mental boundaries way beyond their current positions, always extending yourself outward to accepting greater and greater possibilities. Practice, practice, practice and let nothing and no one stop your imagination.'"

Q. How may I work more closely with nature?

"Ask that you be guided in your planting and harvesting times to bring in the Light. Speak directly to the various devas that are in charge of the crops you're planting. Ask what you can do to assist them, and they will tell you. They will give you instructions on watering and where best to plant the seeds. If you choose to attune yourself closely with them, you can even speak to and control pesky insects, usually by giving them an allotment of land as their own to feed from and play in.

Honor them, for they honor you. By your consciously connecting with the rhythm in nature, you will attract further, more detailed help, precisely when you need it. By this, we mean you will be able to learn techniques on how to grow larger fruit, or have a greater yield at harvest time.

For now, start to think in the direction of co-creative gardening and see what messages you begin to receive from your garden devas. A whole new vista of possibilities await your awareness. Welcome to this world."

Q. Sreper, why am I suddenly interested in growing herbs and using them in cooking? Why do I want to eat more fresh fruit and vegetables?

"We say this is an inner calling from the devas. They fill you up with ideas and inspire you to do all sorts of beautiful things for you and your body. They always hold the sole purpose of loving you, healing you and making your journey on the planet joyful.

Your heart has started to open and this has begun to manifest as an interest in the many 'fruits of the Earth,' such as the herbs, the flowers, the essences of the flowers, the nectar of the various trees and plants, and how you might co-create with them. And, we might add, you miss the nature spirits. Your heart knows the relationship you once had with the little ones... how complete you felt... how much fun you had. As you awaken now, you yearn for that connection.

Reacquainting yourselves with the nature spirits is fulfilling and, indeed, fills you with Love and Light, a quality too often missing on your physical plane.

And, so they want to say to you, 'We love you and we remember you. Remember us who walk beside you. Say hello to your rose bush. Say thanks to the fruit trees, from apples to zucchini. Hug your shade trees. We are there and hear your every word.'"

Energy

"Do not pray for tasks equal to your powers.
Pray for power equal to your tasks." -Phillips Brooks

This dictation was taken outdoors at Lake Ivanhoe, Wisconsin a couple of summers ago. The language and energy was distinctively different than that of my normal practice indoors at my computer. Listening to the angels speak to me in nature was very experiential. I saw and felt their presence.

Q. Sreper, where does energy come from?

"Energy comes from the Creator (the one Source which is referred to by many names) and Who is at the center of Creation.

We say unto you that *energy is everything, and everything is energy.* It is what holds the universe together. It is the glue, if you will, that bonds everything in Divine orchestration... in perfect, Divine harmony."

Q. How does one cultivate more energy?

"We say you cultivate more energy by your personal focus and intent. Focus on creating more energy and you create more energy. Think it and believe it. Desire it, and you will see ways open you can get more energy, and also ways in which to bring it into your life.

For example, manifesting more energy is the same thing as, say, wanting more natural beauty in your life. Humans need to be in nature more often, to immerse themselves in its richness... as you are observing the dragonfly right now before you... flying above the rich green grass.

We say it is important to you, who reside in Earth, to spend more time in nature where your energy field is higher, and we (who dwell in the higher realms) are there with you. It is where you are more keenly aware of our presence.

Take the following thoughts into your heart as you let go and relax..."

A Meditation To Create Energy

"See the cycle of life... all of life. See the bigger picture. Desire, feel, see... touch, have, be. Make it real. Desire, have, be. Make what you desire as real as you can, and let it be. Then, remove the blocks that stand in the way of this new and relaxed awareness.

Enjoy the love you have been given, and give it back. Give more love than you think you have. Open your heart to a new song. Sing your song of love, Dear Ones, and let the world hear it sung! You carry a missing note that the world needs to hear. We say unto you, this day is here for you to sing. Sing your song proudly, eloquently, loudly. Sing it now and let your hearts be free. Rejoice in the energy you give each other. It is God's gift to you.

Many stand in the shadows waiting to see the sunshine. You are the way-showers, the ones who carry the key to unlock their deepest yearning. The golden key, indeed is given you to use now. Rejoice in the energy that you have been given.

Your love is your energy. Your love is your gift. Accept it now and let it shine. Peace be yours for you have worked hard for peace. Your fulfillment is at hand. Rejoice indeed, for there is no more sorrow. This is the energy your love has created. The only thing left for you to do is see it, believe it and accept it. It is yours!"

Q. Positive energy seems to create just as much pressure as negative energy, and we would prefer having a break-through rather than a break-down! How can we best handle this new energy that is coming to Earth?

"We say, those of you who would read our words and listen with your hearts to what we say could never be lost in fearful, human dramas. We ask you to learn to fully relinquish all fears about bodily safety, for you are not your body. When this play is over, and all the props dissolved, you will lighten up so much that you will wonder why you took yourselves so seriously.

Learn to center yourselves in the Light - the Sun - which is the Source of life through which all things bright and beautiful come to you, giving you everything you need for your experience there Is that not enough? What is it that you think you lack if God has freely given everything to you? What is it that you fear?

We say you must learn to give up, one-by-one, all ideas you have ever held of harm and destruction, of evil and death, for in truth these things do not exist. Stop focusing your energy on these things, for it is your focus that feeds its creation. If you think about something long enough, it will manifest. This is the rule of your universe.

We have said this before and we say it again... your world is an illusion. Your world is one where many planes seem to overlap in the same space and time. You can have whatever you want. You can experience anything that you want. Just become conscious of what it is you want. Direct your intention and energy on seeing it, hearing it, having it, and accepting it unto yourself.

Stop adding fuel to the flames of fear. This is indeed the hell of your dark forefathers who didn't know they had the gift of Light so freely given them. Their dark footprints still pave a path on Earth and we say forgive them and let this go. You are still in what we refer to as "the dark age," but you can now make a commitment to the Light, and the Light will come.

This is new to you and we see that even breaking old habits stirs up fear in humans, but do it anyway! The lesson is to go forward through your fears now. Take charge of them.

By facing the enemy, you face your fears, and as you do, they dismantle and disappear just as darkness vanishes the moment you turn on a light switch.

Fear may seem to have its hold on planet Earth and on you, but that is merely an illusion held in place only in your mind. Fear has no reality at all except where you would energize it by your thoughts.

So, let go of these dark ideas and fearful thought-forms. Step into the Light of Love where shadows cannot linger. Forever is a long, long time. Wouldn't you rather spend it reveling in joy and peace?

Come now, and leave your dark toys behind. They are there for your choosing, yes, as it is what makes your world of learning complete on that plane. It is after all, a world of contrast, a world of both dark and light, but it is also a world of choice.

Choose darkness and there is no room for Light. Choose Light and you will wonder, "Where did the darkness go?" Do not forget you hold the power to choose."

Q. What can I do to be grounded and not take on other people's energy?

"We say protect yourself by taking the following steps:

1) Ask for the Great White Light to protect you before you start your day.

97

2) Shed any excess energy that may have accumulated during a talk with a friend.

3) Increase your vibratory rate through prayer and meditation and anyone who resonates at a lower level will leave your life. They will no longer be drawn to you or your energy field because you will be at different vibrations due to the Universal Law of like attracts like.

4) Stay in your own personal power. Do not allow others to pull your energy off center. Do not give your personal power away to drugs, alcohol or other depleting substances. Example: Don't do something you don't want to do just because someone asked you to, or they need you to, or put you on a guilt trip if you don't.

Our Love and Light is with you always. It is in the air you breathe. Call upon us and we fly above you making clear your way. We wish to keep you fully energized with the Light of the Creator. Shine brightly, Dear Ones."

Expectant Mothers

"Life gives you surprises, and surprises give you life." -Unknown

Q. In the past I have lost two children during pregnancy. I am pregnant again and am worried that I could lose this baby too. Please help me!

"We say unto you, Dear One, communicate with your unborn baby's spirit to welcome him or her into your family and into the world. Your baby, though not yet born, is still a spirit who senses the emotions of the people in the world into which he/she is entering.

We say, talk to your unborn baby and express your love. Make your baby feel as welcome as you can, for it can be quite frightening to come into the world feeling alone. To be inspired, imagine yourself as the incoming soul. Coming into life can be scary.

Talk softly and lovingly to your unborn baby. Welcome him or her to the world and feel what a difference that makes. We say this will end your worry. Here is a prayer from an angel to an angel, that we say may help."

Welcome to Planet Earth Prayer

"Welcome to the world,
Dearest Child of God
Whose sweet love you represent.
Thank you for coming here
to be a part of our lives forever.
Beyond this life where you were not long ago
the Light shines brightly still,
and now you bring that Light to us.
Dear sweet child, little Light-bearer of God,
we pray you keep that Light and purity forever,
and remember, that it is always bright within you

no matter how dim the outer world becomes.
And, as you live the life unfolding before you
we ask God to shine upon you every day
as the Sun to keep you safe
within His golden rays of Love.

Dear child, bless you for coming here.
We love you for coming here.
Welcome to the world,
our precious little one. Amen."

Extraterrestrials

"Be not forgetful to entertain strangers: for thereby some
have entertained angels unawares." - Hebrews 13:2

*Q. What are we to make of UFOs and all the current talk
and media awareness regarding them?*

"We see that many people in your Earth plane have had
an experience with extraterrestrial beings, as you call them.
The highly irregular nature of these visits, is that they are
not common occurrences. That makes them frightening to
you. Whenever something is not clearly understood, it is
feared. It is our wish to shed more Light on this for you, so
your fears can be diminished.

Although humans are most curious, you aren't the only
ones having life and form in your galaxy. We ask you to
know and accept the fact that creation goes on forever, even
though it is not all visible to your eyes, or incomprehensible
to your minds.

In all of Creation, there are some who are, let's say, further advanced than you can yet imagine. They have been
able to conquer outer space travel by developing a science
of vehicles, fuels and technology that is so alien to your
minds, we cannot explain it using your limited language.
Some of these beings are so advanced from where you
humans are in your evolvement, that it would do no good to
explain it at this time.

This is not to be a comparison either, for you and every
other being, in every dimension, in every galaxy are always
exactly where they are in the Divine order and unfoldment
of things. All will be understood in its own time. What you
need to be aware of is that you are, indeed, being visited by
other beings from other galaxies and from other dimensions."

Q. What is the purpose of extraterrestrial contacts? Are they to be feared? Are they here to help us or hurt us?

"They come to Earth for several reasons. They are curious, just as you are. They are also here to guide and instruct the Lightworkers of Terra who have volunteered to help this planet move into the next dimension.

Earth is raising its vibrations to the higher frequency of Love, Dear Ones, planet Earth is becoming a Star! Many want to observe this remarkable event. It is not often that a planet 'graduates into the Light.' We could liken the event to your Fourth of July celebrations – explosions of Light in breathtaking colors and loads of excitement. We say that everyone wants to see such a spectacular event.

Some extraterrestrials are here because they are under a contract, of sorts, to help guide humanity into its next evolutionary step. Some of these beings are experts, mid-wives, if you will, having helped many other planets emerge into Light before this. They are being called here to oversee and help where necessary.

Then, of course, there are others whose eyes are on the event for the pure excitement of it. They come to watch, to play, and have fun. These are the ones who could be mischievous and are to be watched carefully. Free will is still the rule upon planet Earth. Anything goes.

But those who are of the Light have come together and still come in droves to eliminate all possibility of darkness. The Golden Rays have interwoven their strands of Light around and through the Mother Earth, and the Love humanity feels for her has kept the dark ones at bay. We see that if this trend continues to hold the planet safe, there is nothing to fear from just a few 'juvenile ETs.' They will eventually join with the Light too.

What is to be feared is your own fear! Remember, like

attracts like. Keep the Love and Light of God in your heart always and no darkness can come upon you.

Keep yourself guarded and protected with a shining ray of Golden Light and beings, from wherever they hail, must honor your command."

Faith

"Have faith everything is all right." - Gurumayi Chidvilasananda

Q. Sreper, what can we expect to have happen when we let go of fear and demonstrate full faith in the outworking of God's Grace and ultimate Good?

"We bring you good tidings of great joy. Those whose hearts are open shall receive their heart's desires. The Light has come. You no longer need to wait its arrival by praying for it, or by earning it by some merit or special favor. It is truly time to release all negative notions held about this.

This is a time of cleansing and releasing any no longer useful thought patterns and beliefs. We ask that you learn to stop yourselves in mid-thought if need be to ask yourself if what you are thinking right now actually manifested right now, would it bring you joy? If not, don't think it.

You have been invited to join with the Light or remain in darkness, it is your individual choice. Dear Ones, we say there will be relatively few warnings about this anymore. Act One begins. Decisions have been made. Those who will lead are the ones who have volunteered to serve the Light and they prepare the way for those who will follow later.

This is not to be interpreted as though one group is better than another group, or will be left behind, for some have simply chosen to stay back awhile, whatever their reason. They will decide and complete whatever is incomplete in their Earth journey, and follow after them, and until everyone has been redeemed and lifted to the next plane in consciousness.

This can be seen as a beautiful unfoldment process that lies ahead for every being. It is not to be feared, for fear is what is being weeded out and left behind now. There is no use for fear where you travel next.

We say unto you that if letting go of fear is fearful, then this next stage will seem fearful to you who hold that perception. But please know that this is the time of graduation from fear. From your point-of-view you will see everything happen - the full spectrum of emotions shall be played out but in very condensed measure because it seems that time is running short - like people arriving too late at the box office and in a big hurry to get the ticket and get seated before the show begins. A 'mad house,' if you will, but without madness. We see it as Divine Order at an intense speed.

Be forewarned that there is no need to panic. You won't miss anything. Your future can't go without you, and you won't miss the opening act because you are the opening act. Use the intensified energies to further define and refine your life's purpose, and stay focused on that mission. You shall have that extra measure of energy needed to accomplish many things that before seemed impossible – even in your imaginations.

Many miracles shall unfold to you. Many hearts will be uplifted and gifted with love. An energy surge of great measure shall fill up the spaces left by the weeding of your emotional gardens. New seeds shall be planted, for the old shall be no more. This is the time of completion of fear, and the contemplation of new visions.

You need to redefine your goals and values and learn how to bring them into reality. It's time for the elimination of fears and forgiving all self-inflicted judgments. These are the prison walls you have built and maintained, but now need to let down the guard. Your minds and hearts shall soar to brand new heights you have not dreamed possible before now.

Planet Earth shall be impacted by this Light. More souls than ever before, including those who have previously passed over the threshold you call death, shall be sending a Great White Light into the heart of the planet via the heart of man.

Envision this as a spotlight beam on the stage. Those with eyes to see shall see, and those with ears shall hear the music of the angels and the song of the Heavenly spheres. Those who are ready will see and/or hear these glorious things, and those who are not, simply will continue to walk in blindness of this Light.

Do not sit in judgment of those who do not join, for in judging, you shall deplete your energy and hold your growth at bay. Instead, catch yourself and ask that the habit of judging cease. Ask for the Light of God to be given and allow this Light to flow into your heart and to expand and radiate outward – in all directions – to all of mankind. Ask your Heavenly Host, your Guardian Angels to release you from fear and imagine yourselves free at last! Your imagination is a powerful source of Light. It is but a glimmer of Heaven itself with more to be showered upon you as you are ready for that vibration to enlighten you fully.

Yes, Dear Ones, this is the time for all great promises to manifest and we say to you embrace this intense Light beaming forth from Heaven. Accept this love and you shall live in joy and freedom forever. We ask that you simply open your heart of hearts and demonstrate the gift of radiant faith.

Fear

"Fear is the cause of every disease and love is what will heal it.
Forgiveness is simply the process of letting go of the fear
and allowing love to enter and do its work." -Sreper

Q. Sreper, what is the truth regarding fear? Why do we experience fear?

"In truth, fear is the absence of Love in whatever form you have created it. Fear exists only in the minds who have created it and given it their power. Remember, fear is not of God, and what is not of God is not real. God is Love, and God is everywhere, and where Love is, fear cannot be.

We say that fear is a teacher on your plane of reality. Without fear as a motivator, you would not accomplish much on Earth. We say it is your job to learn how to move through fear and yet not make a career out of this job!

Let us begin by saying that if you did not see in terms of black-and-white, you would not know the difference between one thing and another thing, for everything would be one shade of gray. If there were no scale of musical notes, there would only be but one sound to hear. If there were but one shape in your world of form, there would be no difference between one object and another. Instead, you have variations of colors, sounds, textures, shapes, experiences, ad infinitum.

And why is this so? So that your experience will be full. So that you can behold all things, for every thing in the manifest world has its own shape, vibration, and color. These qualities are likewise given to non-physical objects, namely your emotions. Indeed, your fears and emotions have their own vibratory rate and color too. There isn't a single being residing in the Earth that does not hold a fear of some sort somewhere within him or herself – or they would not be on Earth. Fear is like a passport to that plane, and overcoming fear is the reason why you reside in Earth. The lesson the fear represents is the premise upon which your life is based. Let us explain.

We see a person near you who is afraid of freedom and independence because that means she must stand her ground and take 100 percent responsibility for her life, paying her own way. Her greatest dream is to be independent and free, yet this is also her greatest fear. The lesson is the same as what was presented in her past and now again, in this present life, she faces it. To those of you in human form it may seem a ruthless journey to repeat the same lesson again and again. You might ask, why is this one's life so filled with such contrast, such pain and fear?

We say unto you that what appears to be a harsh and relentless lesson is but a key to freedom and the gateway to happiness. She must breathe in trust - deeply - and pass over the threshold of change that is standing before her, knowing that when she arrives on the other side of this doorway, all of her life shall be renewed. She will have all the good she has dreamed of having and more. There shall be a showering from Heaven upon her, for she will have finally released the fear that was blocking her and holding her back.

The celebration of life will truly begin and all the world shall behold a new joy in her. The world awaits this dawn of this rebirth like a woman with child waits, for in this triumphant awakening, a path is cut like a machete chops a clearing through a thick jungle. And where this passageway is cut, many wait to enter, making it easier for those who follow after the one who blazed the trail.

So, Dear Ones, rise above the fear in your lives and see the blessing beyond it. Where you see fear, simply acknowledge its presence by directly speaking to it. Do not run from it, deny it, bury it or try to hide from it, but know that it comes as a gift. See past the gift wrappings. Speak from your heart and ask for its message to you. Be diligent and still and hear its only answer.

This is your key for moving through the doorway called fear and into peace. Surrender to The Great White Light all your littleness and excuses that only bring more fear. Indeed, we say give up being scared for being sacred! Changing these little words around makes a big shift in your consciousness. It turns fear into a blessing. That is the reason you have fear on your plane of reality, the place we refer to as Earth School.

Radiate love from your hearts into the world and there will never be room for fear to manifest again. Acknowledge and release any fears that impede your journey and you set yourself free."

The angels have explained that before birth, our souls choose to learn certain lessons during the upcoming lifetime on Earth. Sometimes the most effective teaching tool is the physical body. Unless your soul has agreed to experience the limitation of such maladies as blindness, deafness and dumbness, Sreper offers clues as to what may be the cause and cure of them. In some cases, and in varying degrees, these things can be healed. Results will differ from person to person depending on what course their soul has charted for them in this lifetime.

In the healing process, once the fear is faced and forgiven, the symptoms can also disappear. As examples, Sreper talks about healing eyesight and hearing. You may want to apply the principle he outlines to whatever ailment you have.

Q. What can I do to improve my hearing?

"We say that a hearing deficiency stems from a fear you hold about embracing life fully. We ask you, what are you afraid to hear? What did you hear, perhaps in your childhood that was too painful to hear, and so you blocked it out? Answer this truthfully in yourself now and realize that it is you who is holding you back from hearing completely. All that really needs to be done is to release your fear.

God created all beings equal and with full use of all the senses. He certainly does not punish or withhold any of these gifts from you or from anyone, but it is a thought in you that keeps the gift of hearing at a distance. You are on the Earth to partake of life fully and to also bring others to that level of Light and Love within them... after you have opened the door."

Q. What is causing my poor eyesight, and what can I do to see better?

"We ask that you take our words into your heart, where their meaning will be understood, and then we ask you, what are you afraid to see? Perhaps there was something in your past, maybe in your childhood, that you didn't want to see and so you closed your eyes. We say there are so many beautiful things awaiting you to see and do if you but let go of the fear.

What you need to do is move the love energy from your heart up to your third eye (located on the forehead between the eyes) so that the two become one vision. You have been spending your energy in combat with yourself. Doesn't the phrase 'fighting for love' resonate in an awkward manner with you? There need not be any fighting at all. Know that your thoughts can heal you.

Remember, it was a thought that started your vision to

fail. We say, allow the Light of God to enter your vision and heal your eyes.

Know in your heart that God responds to every thought you think. See only love and love is all you'll see!

Q. I am afraid people will abandon me. What is behind this fear and how do I release it?

"We say that your fear of abandonment is actually causing you to attract the experience of abandonment. Because of this consciousness, life seemingly leaves you 'abandoned' and without options. It is a reaction that can be stopped if you but make the choice to stop it.

Sending the Love and Light of God to those you love, instead of sending them your fears, is where healing begins... and ends. It is but a simple choice. If you choose to stop feeling abandoned, you will stop feeling abandoned. Focus on the joys of life, for it is in blessing your joys that multiply them. This is what Jesus did with the loaves and fishes."

Q. What do I need to do to feel freedom from fear?

"We say unto you, open your hearts to receive the good Heaven has in store for you. Set your hearts and minds on this one goal and choose to see nothing less than this ever. Dismiss your old ideas of sin, guilt and punishment, for you are the one creating that cycle. No one seeks to harm you but the ghosts of unreleased fears you carry from your past, yet to be forgiven. We say that no one can take them away from you but you.

So, alas, we say unto you, ask and be willing! Ask for the willingness to release what is ailing you and holding you in sadness. Become willing to hear another voice instead of your ego's voice. Hear the one that calls to you from Heavenly heights... the one that has been trying to get your attention.

We say, be still now and listen. As surely as you live within the Heart of God, see God as though He were a sea of air surrounding you, ready to give you everything your heart desires and all of what you ask. Know that it is also His desire to give these things to you. May you accept them now. Ask, become willing and become a grateful recipient. Choose to let your fears go and, poof! – they are gone. The following prayer will help you."

A Prayer to Release Fear

"Dear God, I realize that fear is just my teacher. It leads me to the threshold where I go within to my Source, to reconnect with the Divine element that I truly am, to move through this valley to experiencing the good God would let me have. I ask the Holy Spirit to step in and remove my darkness, and to teach me that fear simply means I've been there, done that... I didn't like it and I don't need to do it again, in this or any other lifetime. I ask to be free, and so I am. Amen."

"Dear Ones, remember, fear is what you have been creating and not what Heaven would give you. Acknowledge and release the fears and very quickly be blessed with the peace you truly want. May peace be in your hearts today and forevermore."

Forgiveness

"If you were going to die soon and had only one phone call
you could make, who would you call and what would you say?
And why are you waiting?" -Stephen Levine

*Q. Sreper, will you teach us how we might be able to let
go of what no longer serves us? It seems that people even
have tremendous trouble releasing whatever causes them
unhappiness. I know of one man, for example, who cannot
forgive his parents for something they did a long time ago
and that seems to hold him in a very sad place. His entire
life has been colored with sadness due to his unforgiving
heart. What do we need to learn about forgiveness?*

"We see that the people on Earth have a great deal of
difficulty releasing things, particularly what we refer to as
'tribal consciousness,' or that which once held a deep and
special meaning to them. If they have an attachment to
something in their past, they will likely have difficulty letting it go. We often see that people have the preferred tendency to look at their past and see what was, instead of
looking ahead to see what could be. There seems to be a fear
about the future, that instead of creating something new and
happy, they would rather hold on to a painful memory. And
whatever a person focuses on is what they will experience.
We can't express that enough.

What we aim to do, and what has become our particular
mission on Earth, is to educate people to understand they
are always in charge of their life. They are in charge of what
they create and in charge of what happens to them even
though they prefer to place blame elsewhere, rather than
taking responsibility for their creations.

To make our point, imagine you are a tube-like vessel
that is made out of a material such as stainless steel, shiny

and clean. During the course of your lifetime we see that you have unconsciously created your life experiences which marred and dulled the surfaces of this vessel.

Now, something happens to cause you to alter the course you are on and you begin to awaken spiritually. Through prayer and mediation you turn within for answers from your higher self. This process is like cleaning and polishing the vessel and the surfaces become shiny and bright once again. Nothing of a lesser vibration can cling to it any longer. Your prayers can be likened to little scrubbing bubbles that remove the dullness left behind from painful experiences you've endured during your life.

We would trust that it's the desire of the human heart to be happy and to let go of all things that cause it sorrow or pain. By asking for our assistance through your prayers, we can help you remove any and all obstacles that stand between you and your peace and happiness. We simply need your desire and spoken intent and we can assist you.

Realize that it could take many Earth years for a person to reach the end result of wanting their pain erased, but remember that it takes Heaven but a mere instant to disappear any unwanted misery. We ask you to simply become aware of any sadness that looms within your heart, or in your life, and be absolutely willing to let go of it.

There is something magical in release. Let go of the worry and concern. As you do, see what happens as your new attitude comes forth. Call upon us and ask that it be removed. Dedicate yourself to the outcome you desire most and allow for that to unfold in ways that may not be your own, and you shall have the peace you desire.

We say the dynamic for this unfoldment of good within your heart (and on the planet) has been set in motion since the beginning of time. It simply needs to be recognized by you and applied in your daily life. We guarantee that the promise of divine happiness has already been fulfilled, demonstrated and secured for you. You need only be willing to let go of love's opposite and let change wash through you. Diligently keep your intention of creating a good and happy life and stay clear in this focus. We wish you a lifetime of experiencing pure joy."

Q. What is keeping me from having a total healing?

"We come at this time to remind you that you own the power to heal you. Your journey has brought you to the harvest time, yet you are cautious because the next steps are new to you. You are standing at the threshold of your dreams and we urge you to take the leap forward. Let us help you release the past that holds you back.

Can you forgive yourself? Believe you are worthy of God's Light and know you exist in His Love. The past is gone and you need never punish yourself again. All you really need do is love yourself, release these thoughts of punishment and be free.

The aches you feel now are merely reminders of a lifetime in which you sought to punish yourself 'in the name of God,' believing that would buy you a ticket to Heaven. But we say unto you that God never ordered punishment on you. It is man who created his own guilt and the punishment that would alleviate his guilt.

We say release this need in you that says you are guilty and have no value, for you have come into life to complete this learning. Do it now. Forgive your belief in unworthiness and release it from you."

Grief

"...for it is in giving that we receive;

in pardoning that we are pardoned;

and it is in dying that we are born to eternal life.

-St. Francis of Assisi

Q. How can we cope with the devastating loss of a loved one through death? Please guide us.

"Listen dear children of God, this is Sreper. I am an Angel of the Great White Light. I am here to tell you that each and every human being is a part of a plan so grand, we ask you to stretch your imagination to see the largest picture possible; to see as we see.

We suggest you visualize the entire Universe in which Earth resides. In this vision you are aware of all the other planets, the sun... and in the night's sky, you see millions of stars twinkling. Now, imagine each of those stars represents another galaxy just as huge as the Milky Way, with planets like yours, with suns and moons, and the eyes on them see millions of stars in their night sky.

Now, realize that not one of these millions of stars, and not one single planet or sun or moon is out of synchronization with the rest of Creation. Not one orbiting sphere interferes with another. You do not have planets crashing into each other. Realize, too, that Love is the force that holds all of this beauty and activity perfectly in place. There are no accidents in consciousness, or in God's Creation.

Love is the bond that holds your life together with your Creator. Love is the substance, the glue, that holds everything in place. Love is all. Love is everything. Love is you. You are nothing less than Love and there is nothing more than Love. Given that you are this perfect Love, and there are no mishaps in space, we can therefore say that all is

Love which is perfectly unfolding without accident.

Death, or leaving the physical plane to "return to Love" on this side, is perfectly planned. It is the same power that creates the planets and stars that gives Itself to this plan. We ask that you understand this bigger design and know that your loved one is always in your heart. See them happy and at peace. They may be quite anxious to hear from you so as to not be forgotten. Rest in peace knowing your loved ones haven't traveled too far away. Keep reaching for the brightest Star, for this is where they are.

We are here to help you understand there are no accidents and no sudden deaths. We say, Dear Ones, everything is a segment of a plan so vastly beautiful you cannot see but a fraction of it at any given moment. Remember that in God's world there is no separation. Death cannot separate you from your loved ones, for you are all One."

Q. Is there anything we can do to release the guilt we feel when a loved one dies?

"Dear Ones, you punish yourselves harshly for things you have no control over. It is as though you are saying to God that your plan is better than His.

We join with you in prayer to ask the Heavenly Hosts that you be given the freedom within your hearts and minds to be released from any and all guilt now. Open your hearts to know that all things happen in Divine order under God's timing, including death.

Reach beyond your sorrow to the bright blue sky and ask for the peace that surpasses all understanding to flood your hearts and minds. Feel yourself drenched with the Golden Light we pour into you. We say that along with this Light shall come your rest.

We remind you that you acted perfectly. You did the best

with the information you had at the time. There isn't another thing you could have done to change the outcome. There is always more to God's plan than what meets your limited viewpoint.

The deceased is released from Earth at the precise time their soul directs them to be released and it has nothing to do with you. The best thing to do is release your loved one and bless them on their journey. You are always connected to them through the heart. They are never too far away from you. The caution here is to let go and know that although your loved one is free to go on, they also send their love to you. When you catch a thought of them, it is they who send you an inter-dimensional 'hello.'

Be at peace with this, for it is a gift. Your loved one made his/her transition and so must you. We say unto you survivors that your loved ones always feel deeply for the pain they have caused you and encourage you to let go of the grief as soon as possible."

In the many private readings I have done over the years for people who have lost loved ones, a stunning theme emerged. Regardless of how quiet or how tragic their deaths, the deceased never wanted their loved ones to grieve, or suffer their loss in any way. Instead, they asked them to celebrate their completion on Earth and to bless their journey into a new life in the next dimension.

They often described the place they were in as "glorious beyond words," and to be sad over their passing was ridiculous if we but knew the joy they felt. Indeed, the only sadness that they felt was when they thought of the loved ones they left behind, and would feel the pain of that loss just as we feel the sadness over losing them. In nearly every reading in which I contacted the deceased, they showed humor and lightness, trying to uplift and make their loved ones smile. In all cases, the spirit of the deceased asked for their loved one's blessing and release, so both could go on.

Here is a collection of some of the messages that came through from the other side:

A friend asked about her deceased friend and mother of two children...

"We say, that your friend wishes to tell you she is okay. In fact, she says, 'I am better than okay. Please stop worrying about me. My body (for lack of another word) is so filled with Light, that I am as light as a feather. Be happy for me, please, and stay sweet. We are friends forever. It was no accident we were friends on Earth for they tell me we go way back in time and into different cultures. I'm happy, but I'm a little unsettled.

It takes some getting used to over here. It is very different in that I do not have all that bulk to carry around. Except for the pain you feel over my leaving the Earth plane, I am happy. They say that I have just completed another round of Earth life and need to rest now. Do not worry about where I am and if I am all right because I am so vibrantly alive here that you actually look pretty pale by comparison.'"

A widow asked for a message from her deceased husband...

"We see your husband has become accustomed to his new life here, and we dare say he is feeling well, happy and fit. He says you won't recognize him! He says he can see the beauty of life. He is like a young child in his activities and his expression. He enjoys the boundless freedom, for his physical body was quite tired out. He said he never thought much about what follows physical death, but he was pleasantly surprised and wonders why on Earth did he ever fear death.

There's no fear here,' he says. He is thrilled at how playful life is. Nothing is serious, heavy or dense. Everything keeps moving, changing and merging with other things and thoughts and it all happens in a perfect order and is so very gorgeous, that it would take your breath away. He no longer doubts the existence of a Supreme Intelligence, and he is amazed at how thoughts are things that he can actually see. He likes to spend time looking at thought forms.

Do not fear coming over here, it is what your dreams are made of and more. Your dreams are the closest you get to this place, so hang on to them. This brings us in very close together. We are all one here. There is no distinction or separation between things. It is a blend, like an artist's painting, where all the colors merge to create new colors.

I am busy here. I help people who are experiencing what I went through when I was on Earth. Usually I am called into the operating rooms of hospitals and help from this perspective in communicating with those 'teetering on the edge of life.' I transmit to them instructions from higher Beings of Light, and translate these messages into a language they can understand. I am on the advisory board, you could say, of helping to decide if a person will stay or leave the Earth. I help transmit the energy for this communication to take place.

I say to you, be patient and love every moment, with every breath you breathe. Look into your heart and know that what is real is within those chambers, and only there is it real. Nothing in the mundane world means anything once you arrive here. What I used to treasure matters not anymore. Love is the only thing that matters, so love to the fullest, with all your heart and send love to everyone.

Spend your time nurturing your body, your mind, your spirit and see the three become one. Revel in that Oneness. It is then you will see and know God is within you, living within your heart. Don't knock yourself out struggling, but go easy on yourself. Nurture and love yourself, for that is what will travel with you when you crossover and join me here. Fill your heart with joy and love and teach only this to everyone you meet, for Love is Heaven's gift to you.

Remember, I am not far from you. Talk to me when your mind is still. Call my name and I will come. Look for me and I am there."

A deceased daughter's message to her mother...
"I'm all right, mom! We are closer now than ever and your love is felt by me over here. I love you and don't want you to grieve over me any more. If only our places were turned around and I was there and you were here, I'm sure that I couldn't understand all of this and let go of you either, but with your love for me, please trust me. You are only letting go of something painful. I will always be near you. It is like the angels are telling you in this message that it is okay to let me go now. I am telling you it's all right. I am still here for you and hear your prayers for me. It aches in my heart to see you suffer and filled with pain and guilt.

I am right next door! Develop your faith and see me there. I wish we could have talked about this before I left but I am saying that you can call me and I can hear you. I can talk to you too when your mind is quiet and at peace. Let me go to that quiet place now and let yourself go there too. God has a plan that involves everyone. We will all be in that same place some day where hearts will ache no more, where lessons are learned and life exams are completed.

We choose our own path, you know. I didn't realize to what extent we played a role in this, or if we had any power over our lives, but we do. We create every second we're alive and even when we are "dead." I am not dead! To you on Earth I am dead, but that's because you cannot see past that dimension. When you come where I am, you will see as God sees.

We look at the emotional turmoil left behind with those in Earth. I can see you and I cry with you. We could all cry a river but we must accept God's Will and know that all things, even death, are for our highest good, even if we don't know why it had to be this way. Trust this, please try to trust this. Let your grief go. Look for ways to color your world. I will see you again. I will welcome you when it is your time to return here."

A sister asks her deceased sister... "Are you happier now? What are you doing? Is there anything that you would like to say to anyone here?"

"I cannot say that I am happier when I see the grief I have left you to suffer. That is why I ask that you release the grief and guilt from you now and look to Heaven instead. We are so close that what you feel, I also feel. Clear skies are always above the rain clouds. See me *there*. I am happy when you are happy, and sad when you are sad. I want us all to grow from this experience. Seeing your hearts filled with happy moments and memories will lift me up as well.

I also have been filled with sorrow too and have been wisely guided to this new understanding I share with you. I am still getting accustomed to this new and beautiful place.

Things are much clearer things when viewed from this level. Everything is so magnificent that I cannot possibly describe the breathtaking beauty of my surroundings. I enjoy being here, but I am saddened when I think of your sadness."

A mother whose son was killed in a shooting asked if there was a message for her...

"We see the grief that your son's leaving has stirred in you and we also see your reluctance to let the anger go. The violent way in which your son left has been difficult for you. He says you have grieved way too much and by your holding anger in your heart, you keep him in place on the other side.

He wishes for you to release your resentment toward the one who fired the shots, as he has done. Do not be angry over this but understand that this was no "accidental" thing. There are no accidents!

We say, your son's soul needed to leave and the one who shot him needed his experience. Their two paths crossed up. It was perfect and he asks that you please accept it. Accept his decision and let go. Send only Love and Light to him where he resides now. If you wonder what he is doing, see him helping the Beings of Light. He helps others cross into the next dimension. Envision him helping people under-stand where they are and what they are going through – especially if they left the Earth plane suddenly like he did.

We see your son as you would see a person visiting the sick at a hospital, so to speak, bringing a Light to their hearts. He tends to people in the hospitals in the etheric realm. This turn of events brings you a very deep lesson in trusting the invisible world beyond the physical. It is time to awaken your connection to all of life, in all the dimensions, and to remember what you have forgotten.

Your son wishes we say to you, "Good night, and not good-bye. Tomorrow, do something that makes you happy. Enter Heaven smiling, and you will fulfill my wish, and yours. Return to Light in your heart first, Dear Ones, then return to Light forever."

A woman was so sad over the death of several loved ones that she couldn't stop crying...

"We are with you in your time of sorrow, and we say unto you that it is okay to cry for as long as you need to. Express your sorrow, but remember, there is a rainbow awaiting you. Remember too, that whatever you focus your energy on will persist. When you are ready to let go of the grief that absorbs you right now, you will be free to focus your energy on things that will create joy in your life.

We encourage you to look at the gifts that have been given you by the deaths of your loved ones. See the silver lining. You are radiant. If only you would take off the dark glasses you are wearing and let yourself shine. You have come a long way and we applaud your journey for we know it has not been an easy one.

But trust there are many bright days ahead. It is the message your departed loved ones give you. They want you to be happy. Embrace their memory and let it fuel your life and give you the strength to do the work your heart longs to do."

As I was healing from my fiance's death, my emotions ran deep. I was torn between visiting the cemetery while also wondering if I could ever stop visiting his grave. Being there would always bring on a tremendous sorrow reminding me of his physical death and the pain I went through around the time of his funeral. I felt closer to him away from there. He lived in my heart, and if I listened closely, as I often did, I could 'talk' to him and hear him answer me. Not sure as to what the correct etiquette was with regard to visiting his grave, I asked Sreper for some enlightenment.

Q. Sreper, how important is it to visit our deceased loved one's grave site?

"We say unto you, please do only that which brings joy to your heart, for that is what also brings your loved ones joy. It is the most important thing that grief teaches you. If going to the graveside brings you joy, then go there, but if you are sad and cry over what was, or if you feel guilty about visiting, then don't go there. This is not disrespectful. Doing things that cause a person pain is disrespectful.

Remember your loved ones in your thoughts. Let their memory live as happy moments in your heart. This is what they want for you, and say unto to you, 'Life is too short to miss a single moment of happiness. Please choose to be happy now. Joy travels far in the world of spirit, and it travels far where you are. I thank you for thinking of us in your prayers and want you to know that I love you.'"

Q. What is the lesson for the survivors of suicide?

"In these matters of the heart, we ask you to exercise your faith for indeed, your faith muscle is being exercised. Perhaps you do not yet realize there are no mistakes in your world. Although this is not apparent to the conscious mind, a soul arrives on the Earth on time, a soul creates or attracts his life's lessons on time, and he leaves the Earth on time. Period. The so-called lesson of suicide is one of karma being completed and love being learned. On the human level, one usually cannot see the pattern to things that happen on Earth as we see them from here. A part of Earth learning is the development of trust, for if you knew why things happen as they do, where would the learning be?

You must certainly trust and never judge the agenda of another's soul but always follow your own soul's path. The soul knows its agenda. It is up to the personality to decide to move through or postpone these lessons, but it will ultimately have to learn them.

Many souls are on the Earth now to complete their postponed lessons from earlier life times. Many choose pain to be their teacher although it need not be so. This is partly the reason there are so many serious illnesses and life-threatening crimes.

And, there is an intensity filling the Earth now. Many souls are eager to complete their karmic debts and move into the Light. In even the safest of neighborhoods there are souls finishing up their leftover tasks."

Q. Sreper, tell us what happens to our pets and other animals when they die?

"We say that animals, particularly your pets, have their purpose to help open the human heart to love. It is much easier for humans to love an animal than another person for the simple reason that animals live in total unconditional love. Animals do not judge. They are made of pure love and can only emanate that which they are.

Become completely quiet and ask in prayer for you to be connected with your beloved pet. Ask to make the connection and ask whatever questions come into your mind. Formulate your own dialogue with them. We see this as a grand new opening for you into the dimension of our sister kingdom. It is a relationship you'll cherish forever.

We leave this thought for you to ponder, that all is One – there is no separation. Your beloved pets are with you now as they were before. They have been great teachers for you, just look at how open your heart is to love. This love can be extended to others, for you have uncovered it within you - thanks to your friends in the animal kingdom.

Keep your heart open, for your pets shall live there still. Be happy for them in their new freedom. Celebrate their life instead of focusing on their passing. That is their wish for you."

Humor

Q. Sreper, how do you suggest we lighten up and not take life so seriously?

"Well, that is an easy question to answer. We say simply, 'Lighten up and do not take life so seriously!' You do have a choice!

As soon as your gaze gets fixed on something, pain instead of humor, for instance, pain becomes so real to you that you see nothing else. Then you forget that you have options and could choose to see the bright side. Remember, two things cannot co-exist in the same space at the same time, nor can two opposing thoughts simultaneously exist in the same mind. Choose the humorous view of life. It is a splendid choice that will serve to invigorate healing and joy in both your spirit and your body.

Focus your thoughts on all the things that bring you joy even if it is for just a moment of the day. Restore your minds to seeing only the blessings of a beautiful, fun-filled day. Leave the dark toys of pain, guilt, sin and sadness go. May the awakened joy that is stirring in you extend into all your affairs and gladden the world.

Fill your life with laughter! Learn to see the humor in life around you. It will make your joy multiply. Let your hearts be forever open to the glorious laughter that abounds in Earth, if you look for it. It is, indeed, the best medicine.

Imagination and Healing

"Imagination is more important than knowledge." -Albert Einstein

"Imagination is the chosen vehicle on the Earth plane that you use to explore the subtle worlds not normally known to you while you are still in the flesh. Did you know you can travel anywhere – on any dimension – and see anything you wish to see just by rendering it in your imagination?

Think of being somewhere and suddenly, you're there! This is how powerful your imagination is.

Here is a practical exercise you can do and people will think you have some sort of magical, 'other worldly' powers. Go outside on a partly cloudy day and choose a small cloud that is by itself in the sky. Ask the Creator, "If it be Thy Will and within Divine harmony with the rest of Creation, I ask for that little cloud to disappear."

Then look directly at that cloud and say, "With the power of the Universe, I demand that you disappear right now." Then watch it disappear.

You will realize just how powerful your thoughts and words really are. If you are able to make clouds disappear, what else are your thoughts creating? We say unto you, wake up your sleepy imagination and become conscious of what it is you are thinking.

Start a daily routine of creative visualization to take you places your mind needs you to go. Your eyes need to occasionally feast on other realities for this refreshes your soul and keeps you vibrantly alive.

Develop a habit of daily meditation. Begin to imagine your life as you want it to be. If you are unhappy, imagine yourself to be happy. Create what real happiness looks like in your imagination. Feel how it would feel. We cannot

wave a magic wand over you to change your life entirely
around to where you want it to be, but you can.

We say use your imagination to get yourself there and
have fun creating with it!"

Inner Child

"What lies before us and what lies behind us are tiny
compared to what lies within us." -Unknown

*Q. Sreper, what is the significance of healing the inner
child?*

"First of all, we say that you are constantly creating
your reality by your thoughts and beliefs. Nothing happens
to you without your soul's consent, even painful things. All
would be completely healed if the human race knew how to
let their hurts and disappointments to roll off of them.

We remind you that your thoughts take time to manifest
on the physical plane. Creation seems to move slowly there.
You have also fallen under the veil of forgetfulness where it
is easy for you to say that you never created such a painful
thing to happen. Many on the Earth plane are in denial over
this and that is why it is so frustrating for us to heal it
because the point of power is within them. They have to
realize that they alone hold the key to freedom but have
been too wrapped up in powerlessness to see it.

The inner child is the essence that is you. This essence
is an extension of God. The inner-self is what we will call
the historic you, that is, the total sum of all of the thought
forms and all of the pieces that have occurred in your life to
create who you are today. Your great lesson now, as you
move into a new consciousness, is in letting go of the past.
Open your hearts and know that all your days of growing up
were exactly perfect according to the blueprint of your life.

This question brings you the opportunity to take back
your power and choose again. History need not repeat itself.
Pain was your tool for learning in the past, but need not be
the catalyst now. The inner child is a painful part of you that
you never fully embraced or even acknowledged. It is the

131

part of you that you out-grew, but never put away. It is that part of you that you hang onto as an excuse to place blame on someone else, to duck responsibility, or to to seek someone's sympathy.

If it is your intention to recapture inner-child pain and save it like you would a trophy, a treasured thing of value, we ask why would you hold onto something that hurts you? Go to higher ground, Dear Ones, and forgive. Let this thing go. Ask your guardian angel to help you understand the bigger picture of your life. This new understanding will bring you peace.

Do not spend your precious time dwelling on your sorrows and painful memories of times long ago past, and stop blaming. It is not why you came to planet Earth. Rejoice in your true radiance, embracing every element of you that makes you you. Learn to love yourself and love your so-called enemies... your parents, the ones who brought your lessons unto you, for they are the ones who loved you so dearly to bring you such great teachings.

Forgive them of their seeming darkness and forgive yourself of your perceived mistakes. Forgive your parents, and know in your heart they did what they did for your soul's growth and benefit. Accept yourself as the Child of God you really are.

Free yourself from judgment of the past and look only to what lies ahead. Your lessons need never be difficult again. Rejoice in your new freedom you find today. It is a great wonder to be in the present moment. We say enjoy it! Peace be unto you."

Karma

"Never sharpen a boomerang." -Unknown

Q. Sreper, what is the meaning of karma, and is it valid?

"Karma is as valid as your belief in it has made it so. We see that there are many in the Earth plane who have stumbled upon the meaning of this word karma, and there are many who wonder if they are doomed or blessed because of something they have done or because of something that was done to them in the past leaving them guilty and powerless.

We say unto you, release what you believe to be your karma now, for it is why you walk the Earth. Karma is simply a learning tool where you are. You are within the framework of karma. As you evolve, you will discover a deeper wisdom underpinning this structure and it will become less confusing to you.

You are finding your way back home and this 'karmic structure' could dissolve in an instant if you were but willing to release the thought in which karma binds you. You could be finished with karma if you would instead focus on grace – that gift of Peace from God.

No one is to stand in judgment of this. It is very important that you open your hearts to accept what is. Do not judge, but release your attachments – past, present or future – that you hold. In doing so you will have a transformation. You will see a new freedom and will be able to let go of the old karmic ties you once believed were real.

Do not fear that you are creating karma, for it is now in your evolution that all karmic debts are being repaid. We are not saying that you can go and cause harm to someone, feel justified and remain debt free. You are on Earth to grow through certain circumstances and be finished with the karma that is no longer needed for your soul's growth. The only way you could do this was to return to the Earth plane. Like one who decides to sign up for college courses, you have called these situations to you for this learning to take place, and it is through that experience that you shall be transformed. This could happen in a moment, or in a moment in an eternity from now, but it happens whenever you choose to forgive the past and release your karmic attraction to it.

Remember, you are on the Earth plane to experience emotions and to expand your consciousness. Your learning is coming to a close now, for you have done it all. You have experienced everything there is to experience on that plane. Some of you are bored and wish to return home to another level of awareness that is new, but familiar to you, where the Light still shines in welcome. Some of you refer to this state of Grace as the Christ Consciousness. Dear Ones, you are ready to return to this, why do you not let go of your so-called karma? You are the only one who hangs on to it.

As many of you are aware, many Earth changes are happening. The Light is arriving, and just as though you were to turn on a light switch in a room, when the light comes on, the darkness disappears. We are telling you, Our Dear brothers and sisters in Earth, that the Age of Light and Wisdom shall prevail now. The way for peace and grace is opened unto you.

Choose your actions wisely now, Dear Ones, and after contemplation, we ask you to follow your Golden Rule of, 'Do unto others as you would have them do unto you... now and always.' This will alleviate further manifestation of your attraction to the 'karmic realms.' Behold the Light within and see us there. We say to you, 'Welcome home.'"

Q. I was shot in a robbery attempt. Is the one who shot

me repaying a karmic debt, and is the debt settled?

"Oh, the karmic debts that you humans have stacked up against yourselves! It is priceless what you've paid to be there now to do the things that clear away the rubbish of the past. We dare say unto you, by redirecting your attitude on what karma is all about, you could lighten the karmic load by 95 percent! Your mind cannot believe that it can be karma-free right now and so we give you five percent to keep your mental body happy.

But, Dear One, the truth is that you are already free but your mind keeps the karmic bonds tied tightly around you. We will play along, for this is how the human race has designed life. We like to call your living arrangement 'Earth School,' in which you've been given a certain set of lessons to learn, and just like real school. if you fail a class, you repeat it until you get it.

In this situation, your bonds with your assailant were so intense that it had to be played out in a violent manner. In her mind, she left herself no alternative but to act violently. You see, she has never experienced love. She was raised in fear which was the only emotion ever expressed to her and consequently, this is what she learned. In her violent lifestyle, she acted only on what her violent upbringing dictated to her. Her main belief was, "Get them before they get me!" She was never shown any real love from anyone. No one paid her any attention. When she pulled the trigger that day, she actually wanted to miss you. That act of violence was her unconscious call for help. She wanted to stop her horrible behavior and was crying out to be stopped. She thought that the only way this could happen was to do a violent act and be stopped for good.

We must tell you that her fences were long ago in place. They were already up and around her. She was not a free woman in life before she aimed the gun at you and she isn't a free woman now. The highest thing that you can do is offer forgiveness, knowing that what happened had to be. Accept it fully in your heart as a part of God's Plan. You are, in effect, her jailer and she isn't free until you let her go. You alone hold the key to her freedom. She chose you to lead her out of madness. Do this and the world rejoices, for it will be the end of karma, indeed."

Q. I am curious, who was in my last life that is important for me to know now?

"We say, all those who are in your life were with you, in some capacity, in another life (as you understand it). Some people are 'newcomers' and some have incarnated with you from the very beginning. We say to you that if they did not represent a purpose to you, they would not be in your life. From a person who is no more significant than one you read about in a newspaper, to your dearest and closest friend, we say they all hold special meaning. You have known them before.

There is a karmic connection to this. Also, keep in mind that karma is neutral, it is neither 'good' or 'bad.' It simply means there is something left unfinished from another time. The situation arises again to be 'balanced and canceled-out;' to be forgiven and cleared from your cellular memory so you are free from all karmic bonds.

Love will heal all karma.

We say look any perpetrator straight in the eye and say, 'I forgive you and I appreciate that you bring this to the Light for me to look at and release. The debt is now forgiven. Thank you God that this is so. Amen.'"

Lack and Limitation

"Argue for your limitations, and sure enough
they are yours." -Richard Bach

Q. Sreper, please help me understand why I am experiencing lack and limitation, and how can I stop this and move on to living life abundantly?

"We say unto you, your escapades to the Earth planes have been many and you have always set very high ideals for yourselves. You have hammered away at these goals relentlessly and they have tired you out. We suggest you begin to realize that you are on a 'mission possible,' that in order for you to move forward, you felt you needed to go backward, to retreat into having an experience of limitation. You have momentarily forgotten that you have One Source from which all goodness flows, and through God, you have everything. We come this day to tell you that lack no longer serves a purpose in your lives and you can choose now to let it go. Be done with that lesson and graduate now. Lack and limitation was your teacher, but you are now entering a new school where limitations are no longer the motivation for learning. The learning process you have known on Earth will be obsolete where you are going.

The next dimension of time and space virtually eliminates time and space, allowing you the freedom to exist simultaneously with your thoughts. We say to you that upon thinking them, they shall manifest quickly before your eyes. Earth has been like a practice run. There has been a seeming time-lapse between your thoughts and their subsequent form. You have time to 'change your mind' and redirect your thoughts before they become a reality. We also want to make note that it is important for you to know that you've done nothing wrong in this learning process.

Pick up the pieces you want to take with you and leave the rest. Bless them into oblivion! Then, put the cherries back into the bowl of life and step forward into a new arena of endless joy and abundance. We dare say that you do not lack for anything. It is only in your limited thinking that you feel you have a need. We say look again and see all of the bounty of this Grand Universe and stop putting limits on yourselves. God has placed no limits anywhere. Wherever you have placed a fence and told yourself, 'This is as much as I can have,' think again. Then, open the gate and release yourself. The key is *know who you are* – you are vast and unlimited beings, living in tiny bodies. You are on Earth to experience unlimitedness. This is also God's goal for you.

Bless and release yourselves from your fenced-in yards. Go forward into the Divine unlimitedness and express that in all you do and say. It is natural for you. Rub the sleep from your eyes and awaken, Dear Ones. God gives you thoughts so that you can become more of yourselves and express yourselves fully. We say, He would not inspire you without also giving you the means for manifesting them.

We ask you to listen to our voice speaking within you. Meditate on accepting a new life of abundance now, in whatever way you desire to have it. Allow the universe respond to your prayers. *Expect the unexpected!* You do not know what will come about, nor when, nor where. Your job, if you will, is to find your bliss and follow it, and you shall be lifted over the fences you have built around you.

Allow limitlessness to flow through your life and count the many blessings you already see. A grateful heart is a surefire way to spark even more awareness of God's abundant Universe.

Learning Lessons

*"Watch for big problems for they disguise
big opportunities." -Unknown*

*Q. Sreper, my car was stolen and I would like to know
what lesson is there for me to learn?*

"The lesson in your car being stolen is, in part, a result
of a fear you have of losing your good. You believe that if
you do something 'bad' God will retaliate and take something from you to punish you for your so-called wrongdo-
ing. In order for you to create a more comfortable experience, you must redirect your personal power. We suggest
you decide to end the habit of worry and trust the Universe
to respond to your wishes without the ego's special effects
you felt you needed, things being stolen from you, for
instance. You do not have to grovel, plead, or do something
special to earn the good God has already given to you. You
always have access to everything because that is God's Will
for you. And we might also add that your little will doesn't
stand a chance against His.

Whatever your consciousness is sending out to the Universe will return to you tenfold. If you have been sending
out fear-filled messages, fear will return in any one of its
numerous forms.

Do you believe that no matter what good you acquire in
life, there is someone lurking around the corner to take it
from you? We say unto you, where is your mind? In what
do you have your faith?

We say, stand guard over every thought, word, and
deed. Notice every thought you think and ask yourself, "Is
this something I really want to have happen in my life?"
Whatever you give your mental power to, shows up in your
life sooner or later – good, bad or indifferent – all thought

creates. Choose what you want to create and think only those thoughts.

Remember, whatever it is you are feeling and giving your power to will ultimately become a part of your reality. No one is lying in wait to take your good away from you unless you have first held that belief in your mind. To stop the effects that you do not like from manifesting in your life you need to stop the thinking that creates them.

Write out a new list of goals. Write from your heart each and every day until your mind is retrained in its thinking. Keep a list of all of your accomplishments and all of the little successes you have made on the road toward your goal. We suggest you breathe deeply and relax. Breathe and become clear.

Lack of faith in Divine Goodness is what keeps you awake at night. We say unto you to change your focus completely. See only good in all things, and remember everything that happens to you is coming from Love, or it is a lesson to learn Love. No one is punishing you or keeping your good from you except you and your old belief system that made that possible.

See how powerful you are? The world returns unto you whatever you have asked for, but be patient. Creation moves slowly where you are, but for good reason. Can you imagine, if in all your angry moments, the things you have said would have manifested in an instant?

The slower vibrations in Earth give you a chance to cancel and restate what it is you really want. With this you learn the virtue of patience. The more determined you are, the more definite your decisions, the quicker the manifestation takes place.

The Universe loves a made-up mind! It knows how to respond and bring decisions forth. Affirm what you want with determination, as though your life depended on it, and you shall see things happen very quickly.

We give the following prayer for you to affirm as often as necessary until you feel you are clear and back in your own power again."

A Prayer For Clarity

"From the Lord God of my Being, I release from me any old and worn-out belief I have held since the beginning of time that keeps me from realizing my full potential, my greatest happiness. I succeed in my new goals. Any thought in my mind, and anything in my auric field that is not here in the name of Love and Light, I release from me now. I am clear.

My connection with the Creator is restored. God gives me his certainty now. I have His Highest Thought as my Eternal Guide. I know where I am going. I align with Him and I am free to experience my life fresh and new. I know that the best possible good comes into my life at the perfect moment.

So be it. Amen."

"Say this prayer daily to attune your mind to the new Light that is dawning within your consciousness. This will clear you and keep you clear."

Letting Go

"To give a problem to the Holy Spirit to solve for you means that you want it solved." - A Course In Miracles

Q. My life seems like it's at a stand still and I have no energy to move forward. What is the matter?

"Go within yourself and ask what would bring you the gift of true joy. What is it that you have always wanted to do but had more excuses than personal drive to accomplish it? We say, release all excuses and step forward toward your goal. Let go, let go, let go! There isn't a better time for you to do this than right now.

All things are continually being made anew. Do not let yourself cling to old ideas, and do not compare yourself to what others are doing. What others do is none of your business. This type of thinking is stagnant and only serves to pull you down. You are there to do your thing and we say *do it*. Stop comparing what is happening now to what happened in the past.

Step ahead into the future and follow what is inside your heart. Listen to what your heart tells you. This is a lesson in trust, which is a part of your soul's curriculum. In doing this, you always have the energy you need to accomplish a goal. Do not let your past thoughts block you in any way, for this is what makes your trek upon Earth difficult.

Bring the Love that God abundantly supplies to you into you, and you will always have His vibrant energy to live your life. Ask for your heart to guide you in letting go of what is no longer needed, and release it like you would excess baggage on a hike up a mountain trail."

Light

"What is to give light must endure burning." -Victor Frank

Q. Whenever something good happens, why does something bad also happen?

"We say you must totally come into the Light of God where no darkness is or ever could be. If you choose to put your trust and faith into what you term "bad," you shall continue to create darkness for yourself. We invite you to come into the Light fully and fear not the darkness you think you see, for it is only a shadow that vanishes into Light. Evil is but an illusion created in the active imagination of man's mind that isn't any more real than a nightmare a child has while he is asleep. When the child awakens, the nightmare disappears. We say unto you that your soul wishes to finally dismiss all nightmares from your reality.

This is what you term the inner battle of Armageddon, the battle of Light and dark, of good and evil. Remember, this need not be a battle at all. All you need to do is simply give yourself permission to step fully into the Light and Love of God and dismiss all else from your thinking. Affirm: *"There is only One Power in the Universe and it is Good."*

You stand at Heaven's door and you make the choice whether to enter or not. As you learn to release your beliefs in darkness, one by one, more Light is added to your fire and the brighter you become. Choose once again your goals and Divine Providence is given to you according to your faith. Establish the peace of God within you now and your world reflects peace back to you.

Establish Love within you now – for all of your brothers and sisters – and they will reflect back to you the love you offer them."

A Prayer for Light

"I am born anew this day. I release any and all old, negative beliefs about myself. My life is vibrantly new and alive, and fresh with love in its center – in my center – in which I live and have my being now. I am clear. I am as God created me. I move forward in my life knowing I am the Light I seek. Amen."

"Breathe deeply, breathe very deeply. As you do this beautiful exercise, think only on this – that you breathe in the very substance of Light and Love itself. You breathe in God. And as you breathe, visualize this Light/Love substance going inside your body, into all the darkened chambers and cavities, into all the organs, the rib cage, the heart, the veins, and see your body fill with Light as though you are walking through a beautiful palace flipping on the light switch in every room and passageway. See the brilliance of this Light and meditate on this vision.

Direct this God/Light substance toward the wounds of yesterday. See any pain as darkness vanishing into this Light. Forgive any belief in unworthiness and release it.

Repeat this meditation until your heart believes you are love and beauty and nothing else."

Basking in the Light Meditation

"Stand and look in the direction of the Sun. Close your eyes and imagine the Sun's Light and energy pouring into you. You may feel off-balance momentarily, but stay with it for just a few minutes. Then, hold your hands out facing the sun as if to collect these rays. See the sunlight traveling into your left hand, through your body and out through your right hand. As it leaves the right hand, direct it toward yourself or anyone else who enters your mind who needs this energy for healing something in their body or in their life.

When you sense completion, end this exercise with giving thanks. Know in your heart that what you saw inside your mind's eye has indeed happened in time and space as well. And so it is. Amen."

Lightworkers

"Never doubt that a small group of committed citizens can change the world. Indeed, it's the only thing that has." - Margaret Meade

Q. I am a Lightworker and I have no trouble radiating Light to others, but my own life is in shambles. Why can't I help myself?

"You feel others deserve to have love, but not you. You see yourself facilitating love to them, like a servant serves a feast to a king, hoping you can savor a crumb or two that falls to the floor, but we say this is nonsense! From this plane of reality where we are, we see the river of Love flowing directly through you, as though you are a sieve. What you need to do to hold that energy is to 'patch the holes,' as it were, where God's Love leaks through.

Flight attendants will tell you to place your oxygen mask on you first, then assist someone else. Take in Love for yourself first, then extend Love to someone else.

We say unto you, become a vessel that can hold the Love you not only give, but also seek. Do not be dismayed thinking this need be a long process, or that you do not deserve Love, because if you are on the planet – and you are on the planet – you deserve Love. That is God's Law. And as you share and give your Love to others, you strengthen it within yourself."

Q. How can I best help the people who are in my life?

"We say, you can best help your family and friends by being who you truly are. Stay clear of all influences that deter you from doing what you know is right in your own heart. You help others by being an example. Walk the talk you hear. By being true to yourself, you honor everyone else in Creation with you.

Go into your day now in peace, knowing you are dressed in Glory. You have taken up the work of God Himself, for you hold the deed to His Divine Will. Ask and it is given you. Be guided on your path. It is a narrow one, but we tell you its beauty is unsurpassed.

If the going gets rough, look and see our wings lifting you up, and we trust this will give you rest. For those who give of themselves to others who are temporarily in need, shall be lifted up."

A Prayer for Lightworkers

"I have the power to heal. God has sent me as Himself to do His work on Earth. By His breath, I breathe. By His love, I love and am complete. My desire is to share His Love and Light with all of Creation. I am a Divine Spark and I know it.

I light the lights in those whose flames have flickered and gone out, and one by one, Earth becomes a brighter place. Awakened is the memory of our inheritance of Light. God gives me the strength and knowledge to share share this with those who come to me and ask. So be it. And so it is. Amen."

Living in Harmony
with Planet Earth

"If you keep doing things like you've always done them,
what you'll get is what you've already got." - Unknown

Q. Sreper, what is the importance of living in harmony with planet Earth? It seems that mankind is so far removed from the natural cycle of things that we will never get back in balance. Help!

"To answer this, we must first talk about the importance of the Earth's seasons. We say to you that it is of the utmost importance to become as natural as you can, even if it only be in your heart at first. By that we mean that you are in physical bodies and you dwell on a physical plane and you must align with that environment as best you can in order to be in balance within you and with the world.

If you follow man's manipulations of nature, and for example you eat 'man-made' or altered foods instead of natural ones, your body will be out of balance. The result will be an underlying unhappiness.

Learn to listen to the rhythm of the Earth and get yourself in tune with it. There are natural patterns inherent in nature which you can learn about and follow once again. Find this path home to where you once were. Listen to the lesson of your native forefathers, for they hold the key to this path. They knew how to live in perfect harmony with the elements and so must you learn, for that is where you will find ultimate balance and regain your happy heart.

Without a connection to nature, your lives are without real meaning. There can be no logic to your wanderings and that leads you into living an artificial life which is the source for all unhappiness. Separation is the key to loneliness. Your innate sense of loss stems from not being in the natural flow and natural rhythm of the life that surrounds you. You have forgotten the importance of living a natural life. We say it is time to call yourself home.

We suggest you establish a daily routine where you can quiet your mind and allow your heart to speak. Ask your native forefather's spirit to come into your life and connect with you. Ask for guidance in learning how to live in harmony with the land. Ask, 'What can I do to be more in tune with the natural, rhythmic cycles and stay in balance, even if I live in the midst of a concrete jungle?' Listen for a moment for the response and let yourself be surprised at what is revealed.

Reacquaint yourself with the knowledge the natural cycles of the Earth, the moon, the sun, the stars offer you, for they hold deep meaning. Study and learn from them. Get back to the Earth and let all the artificial stuff go, for it only seeks to complicate your life.

Make a conscious effort to align with nature, even if your contribution is just a prayer in your heart. (Thoughts are real things in our world!) Seek ways to unite in harmony with nature, for it calls you home to a life you were once familiar with. It is true, the olden days are gone, but we say, the connection to nature is never lost and calls to you even now. This is the world you created. Seek to reunite with the natural laws and seek not to change what is, but rather learn to live in balance and cooperation with it."

Meditation

"Your vision will become clear only when you look into your heart.
He who looks outside, dreams. He who looks inside, awakens."

-Carl Jung

Q. How can I meditate deeply and get something valuable from it without dozing off?

"We say unto you that you always gain something from meditating even with your dozing off. Your spirit guides have you active on other dimensions at this time and they have been trying to get you turned around to see and hear all that is happening in your life. In some of your meditations the angels touch your heart with love in order to open you up.

Practice your meditations daily and try many different methods to find the one that suits you. You need not repeat a method that does not seem to do anything for you. Did you know that you could meditate from horseback riding if that is an activity you love to do? Or knitting, painting, golfing, or swimming? Try a walking meditation where your conscious mind is busy with that activity to clear it enough to hear our voice.

The ancient Chinese, for example, believe that 'standing meditation,' along with deep breathing is the most beneficial of all meditations, however, what is the most enjoyable to you is what is best for you."

Murder
and other Acts of Violence

"A new commandment I give unto you, that ye love one another,
as I have loved you." - Jesus, (John 13:34)

Q. Please help me make sense out of all the senseless murders and other such horrible crimes people do unto others?

"Dear Ones who abide within the 'laws of man,' plainly we see, the ego runs rampant in your world. It causes chaos, death and destruction in its path wherever it goes. The Earth plane offers a stage for which it can act out all the gory details of its rampage, with nothing to stop it but the will of man aligned with God. Envision two people fighting, fist to fist, but one decides to no longer fight and so he withdraws his fist. What do you suppose happens with his opponent? What would his fist strike against if no one were there to fight it out with him?

The Earth plane gives audience to the acting out of all the ego whims because the ego is excitement on your plane. God did not make it so, you did. The ego's job was to merely keep you safe from harm while you were in a body, but your minds have given it power to rule over you, and over God. To make sense out of senselessness we go to God and His Messenger, the Holy Spirit. We ask Him to remove our fascination with such things as murder, rape and violence. We ask God to get inside the human heart and wipe it clean. We ask God to turn our heads away from such violence, and give us peace.

Dear God, restore Your plan on Earth, for we have lost our way. If this is Karma working itself out, it is of the ego and we must exercise forgiveness now. May we all be inspired to do what is right, onto ourselves and onto our brothers and sisters who share the planet with us. May we all want Peace and Love more than anything else. Instilling everlasting Peace on Earth could be easy to do, as it is what God has also willed for you.

Each and every day, denounce the ego's whims and reach to God as your Guiding Light, and align yourself to Him. See as God sees; love as God loves, and you cannot hurt your neighbors who are one with you.

Go into your day and send God's Love and Light before you, then watch a miracle happen! You can defuse each and every 'hot spot' you find yourself in, or are a witness to, with Love as your shield. Ask your Guardian Angel for the words to say to deflate the ego and diminish the issue, then you be first to step into the middle of the ring, and lower your fist.

Contemplate for a moment your prisons. You have convicts who are serving time behind bars, but you also have jailers who are also doing time behind bars, on the other side of the bars! It takes two to tango, as they say. We ask you, *who* is in prison? They both are! And their ego minds have placed them there.

We propose to you in this new age of Love and Light, to stop talking about forgiveness and practice forgiveness! There is no degree of difficulty in miracles. From having a thought as small as low self worth, to murdering someone, it is all of the ego and not of God. Maybe it would be easier for you to start small, by truly forgiving yourself of all your self-judgments that hold you in hell and behind your self-made prison, and then forgiving those who seem to be attacking you, and holding you there.

Arrest this critical nature of the ego now! Set yourself free to live a life of joy and bliss! Stop playing the ego's game. It's not Karma anymore, it's ego, and with the Almighty Power of Heaven, the ego must be undone. The time is now and Heaven is here to help you.

News Media: Part One
The Roles of the Sexes

"Remember, Ginger Rogers did everything that Fred Astaire did,
but she did it backwards and in high heels." -Faith Whittlesey

*Q. Sreper, there seems to be a lot of activity in the Earth
these days regarding the roles of the sexes, particularly how
women's roles are changing. What is woman's purpose
and/or mission on Earth? What does this really mean?*

"We would be happy to shed some light on the female
role for you. We say that the roles appear to change because
your perception of the female and male sexes, along with
their duties as it were, has changed. As you grow and evolve
and your life unfolds, your roles adapt and change and you
emerge anew.

We say that, collectively, as a human race, much evolvement and change is occurring in women everywhere and the
thrust of this change has been brought to the forefront and
into consciousness namely because of the media on the
planet. Indeed, every issue facing man is amplified and glo-
rified through the use of Earth's loudspeaker system, namely the news media.

We say unto you that you are not just dealing with the
core issues within your own personal being, but you also
face the pressures of resolving all issues everywhere
because they are continually put in front of you via your TV
and radio networks, the Internet, or in your daily newspa-
pers. It seems a difficult task to escape these tremendous tri-
als and tribulations facing human beings, the issues in your
own back yard, in your hemisphere, or around the world.

The media brings you the culmination of human suffering right to your doorstep and into your consciousness,

regardless of where it exists on Earth. The despair and anguish of the world is your constant companion. It is with you when you eat. It sleeps with you at night. It is written into your subconscious minds and becomes the soundtrack you have learned to dance and move your life to. This is why it is so very important you seek refuge through quiet time and meditation.

Equally important is engaging in an activity you thoroughly enjoy and involve yourself, on a daily basis. Clear your hearts and minds of the world's woes and go within to the peaceful state you know and love but has been shoved aside by the wails of the world. Instead of agonizing along with the newsreels, or complaining, 'Oh well, what can I do about it?,' we say, take yet another step, higher and away from all that noise. Seek to know what is in your heart and make that the reality in which you walk.

It's quite a simple plan and easier to do than you think. To experience peace, become peaceful. To experience love, become loving. Release mass-consciousness from you. Let the world be witness to your new self and the new life you've chosen to live, the life of peace, the experience of love. Keep this effort alive. Do not doubt that past efforts have been in vain, for great new light is pouring into Earth through the human heart open to receive it.

Much, indeed, has been accomplished! It's just that you hear little about it because the focus of the human ego still has your power and is still insisting on pain and suffering of the past rather than allowing you to recognize the spirit of love welling up inside you.

We say unto you that if you so desire, you could change your world completely in a heartbeat. Insist on seeing peace instead of what the broadcasters so willingly shout to the world. This is the ego's distraction. But you do not need to buy into its doom and gloom any longer. The ego's ploy is to steal you away from peace and keep you powerless in a sad and lonely place.

Lift your heads higher, dear ones and hear our words. The female role has always been to embody love. Her purpose was to bring love into form and love without conditions. This is not to say she was "second" to man as your world has basically taught you to believe, for all human beings are created equal.

There are differences in your world of form because there are different purposes for being in that world. Women unconsciously chose to suffer under the dominion of her male counterpart by giving her power over to him, while he has also gladly taken it. Now comes the wake-up call. Women are realizing what they have done and they are coming out of their sleep to reclaim what they had given.

You see this as a 'new movement,' but we say it is but a continuation of one long drama, merely an act in the play, where the female is reclaiming the power she had misplaced. She is returning home to the heart. She brings with her the curiosity of the world of man, who suddenly feels threatened at her newfound strength and will, but we reassure him he has nothing to fear and the world to gain.

The job here and now is to relinquish fear and stop the battle. Know this is God's Divine Plan unfolding. Woman is emerging into herself. Imagine life on the planet bathed in the warmth of mother's love and nurturing care. Imagine how different the world could be and better than what it has been thus far.

Welcome yourselves home to the heart of the hearth, and embrace the goddess as she moves through your life. Seek only the beauty she brings in the days that lie ahead and you shall never again feel the fear the ego would hold you a prisoner in. Seek the higher ground of abundant, radiant love so bright that the world sees not another shadow. If just one heart awakens today, truly awakens and lets fear go, the world would emerge into Light fully and completely.

So be it. Celebrate your love and light on this new dawn. Embrace the female energy in all beings, for it is indeed in all beings regardless of their sex. You have all been both sexes at one time or another and now is the time to remember your Oneness. Do not deny that which needs to emerge and express, for it would be denying a great part of your experience, and denying the very reasons you have come to Earth at this time. Be at peace, and show your love to one another always."

News Media: Part Two
The Link to Stress

"It is easier to protect your feet with slippers than to carpet
the whole of the earth." -Unknown

*Q. There always seems to be so much negativity going
on in the world that it is difficult to cope with life. How can
we best view and understand events that cause us stress,
such as mass suicides and earthquakes?*

"We say unto you that life in Earth can be challenging
to you who do not know the full realization of all the mind-
ful experimentation that is taking place on that plane.
Remember that Earth is but a classroom... several million
classrooms actually, where everyone is busy learning a mul-
titude of lessons.

What is challenging you is the fact that you live in a
time of great communication and devices that enable you to
be literally hooked into every event that happens. You hear
about it within moments of it happening! All you need do is
turn on your TV or radio, and you hear about someone
else's woes, in your back yard or in a neighborhood on the
other side of the planet, not to mention the grand attention
given to negative, sensational news such as that of the mass
suicide. This causes great stress on your bodies that are not
designed to take on the woes of the world.

We say unto you, it is in your best interest to withhold
your personal judgment of such events for you cannot see
the entire picture of what goes on in the minds and hearts of
other people who are also on the planet to learn what they
are there to learn. Anytime you're a witness to such an
ordeal, remember that you can only see a small fraction of
the entire scenario and so we warn you, do not judge. Judg-

ment holds you from reaching higher thresholds. Judging keeps forgiveness from your heart and locks it away in pain.

You cannot possibly know, from where you stand and look outward on the world, what goes on in the minds of others, nor can you try to figure out why they do what they do, or why they don't do what they don't do. You humans waste far too much mental energy on needless worry. Instead, why not spend your time keeping your focus on yourself?

If you should find yourself judging someone else, ask to be released of it and be led to higher ground. Seek to know the bigger picture of any event that has your attention, and then send your love to it. Bless it into oblivion. How long do you need to do this? We say, "Until you have no more situations that are drawing your attention to it and away from your inner peace. If you're distracted by outer events of the world, we say to bless it and release it. Draw none of this negativity unto yourself, either from witnessing or judging. Would you not prefer to enter into pure White Light and live a more refined existence where darkness is no longer your companion? Where it evaporates as a mist in the sun's golden rays and draws you ever higher into it?

What a thrill this is waiting in front of you to behold and experience! No longer will you run and hide away from love but will choose to face whatever 'demon' faces you instead. Bless it into the mists and allow the Light of day to evaporate it into nothingness. Be a savior. Set the example. Remember, you need to release it as it also needs your releasing.

Let all judgments cease at this time. We say that those involved in this suicide, as in every other event that happens in time and space, were not random victims but willing participants who chose this destiny for themselves. Every soul in human flesh chooses their fate whether they are fully aware of it or not, or whether you are fully aware of it or not. But you are not there without help from the higher planes.

We say to you that the angels are here in force now and always, to encourage and guide you into making better choices for yourselves. Please remember that pain and suffering are mere options in an array of millions. Look to higher ground, dear ones. Call us into your consciousness, and choose a higher path."

Pain and Suffering... Why?

"Trust that all things happen for a very good reason." -Sreper

Q. Why do we choose to incarnate on Earth to learn lessons if we are already perfect?What is the purpose of human suffering and is there a good reason for it?

"Ah, but suffering exists only in the mind of the one who suffers! We say that you have forgotten that you have choice on that plane. We say that you can, at any time, end suffering and turn away from it forever. You can, right now, choose Love and Light and Peace instead, and know in your heart that whenever a painful thought enters your mind you can deny it power, demand that it leave, and focus on love and peace instead.

The 'fall from Grace,' as it has been termed by humanity, has happened so long ago you haven't but the faintest glimmer of what life was like before it. We are speaking of life in your True Reality, in what the Christians call 'Heaven.' Now, we say that the purpose for suffering is a scheme set-up by the human mind to get your attention in order for you to wake up and change your focus back to what is Real... God, Love, Peace, Joy, Harmony, Oneness, etc. Humanity has been delving deeply into darkness, far away from the Light of Spirit from which he came. To see this as we see it, stand facing the sunshine for a moment and then turn your back to it. Do you not see shadows? This is the position you have been in since the fall and have become lost in the mystical illusion, thinking these shadows are real.

And now we come to remind you that the Light is here, indeed, it never left. Turn around once again and see your way home. Whenever you decide you're finished playing in the elements with your destructive toys you may return to the Light. We say the choice has always been up to you but has been forgotten in the shadows of your mis-creating."

Q. Why are our lessons often painful?

"We say, your lessons need never be painful. You have options. This is seen as quite an undoing of your belief system. It is a mental habit that has become ingrained in your mind. To change this experience of painful lessons, change the consciousness that creates or attracts these experiences. Pain comes to you as a teacher and knocks upon your door of physical reality until it gets your attention. It calls out to you as a friend who says, "Change your thinking and you will stop hurting."

You have choices and we say to choose again. Lighten up, as it were, and release these thoughts. Change your habits and change the outcomes. Apply new rules that are based in total love. Learn to love and nourish yourselves. Start your day with a simple three word affirmation, "I am Love." As time goes by, expand that thought of I am Love into adding more sweet words to it and carry them with you throughout your day. For example, "I am Love. Everything is Love. All I see is a reflection of Love." Carry these new thoughts into your sleep state by repeating these statements before retiring at night.

Weed your garden of all critical thinking, for you cannot tolerate the pain these judgments inflict upon you any longer. Give yourselves the Grace of God. When you talk to yourself, talk as you would to your most cherished friend. Call upon your guides who are in spirit to help you. They will join with you in nurturing you, gently reminding you to rise up to your new way of thinking should you wander.

Pain seems real to those who have forgotten they could choose peace instead. It is as simple as remembering you are one with the Creator and all you need do is instill His sweet Love in your heart.

Isn't it true that when you see a child cry, he is able to dry his tears when his mother comes to comfort him? In effect, this is what we are suggesting you do for yourselves to remember that Source of Love is within you. It has always been there. No one comes to the Earth plane without his Divine Connection to Source. Love flows freely to all, for everyone was created equal. Now it is as simple as remembering that connection and putting Love into action.

Physical pain comes to you as a teacher, and you must discern the lesson it brings unto you. Every single being in the human world can learn to listen to their inner voice and determine correct action to take to learn the lesson and be free from pain. Your normal state is bliss. Whenever you find yourself sad or in pain, find the thought, word or deed that started it and pull it out of your consciousness like a weed from a garden. It serves no good purpose to dwell on what caused the disharmony, but correct the thought by replacing it with what you truly want to experience, and move forward.

Those who keep looking back at what was shall be frozen in stone for they will never truly live in the Light of a new day. Ask for the release of pain and we come to assist you. You never walk this way alone."

Parenting

"We spend the first twelve months of our children's lives teaching them to walk and talk, and the next twelve telling them to sit down and shut up." -Phyllis Diller

Q. How can I be a more patient and loving parent?

"We suggest you see your children as perfect expressions of Divine Love. They are on Earth to have their own experience. They are with you because you have chosen them and the experiences they will teach you, as they have also chosen you as their teacher.

See the perfection in this arrangement of being together with them. Your children have chosen lessons to learn in this lifetime and they are in total synchronization with you and your plans, or they would not have come to Earth through you. Know that all things work together for the higher good of every soul involved, in your family and indeed, in every family throughout the world. What takes place in your personal relationships will extend as a Light to people everywhere. Be patient and loving, and that is the energy they will take forth into their world. Teach love and love is what will be instilled in your kids."

Q. How can I best prepare my children for the future?

"You prepare children best by extending Love and by not giving them your fears! We say unto you, be a shining example and remember, your children come as your teacher, too. Teachers and students alternate roles. Act from love. That is what your children will learn from you. What better gift for them to inherit!"

Patience

"Time moves so swiftly with promises of love,
and so slowly between." - Rev. Nancy Freier

Q. Sreper, what is the truth about patience?

"We say impatience is caused by worrying. You spend about 99 percent of your time thinking about what happened yesterday or worrying over what may happen tomorrow, but rarely do you tend to what is going on now. You cannot relive yesterday, nor can you live tomorrow before today.

We say unto you, that you must create a new habit of staying in today, and whenever your mind wanders to another place or time, you must diligently call yourself back to the present moment. It is where all your creative personal power resides. In other words, you are powerless over yesterday and powerless over tomorrow, but if you really accepted the fact that you are powerful right now, you will have mastered patience.

We remind you that time is complicated for us to explain. You are on the Earth so you must do as the earthlings do and obey the law of time and to live one moment at a time, one moment following after another, in a very specific, linear order. With this practice comes order and with order comes the end of confusion which is what causes impatience. Remember, live today and you set yourself free to enjoy each and every one of the moments of your life as they unfold. being impatient makes you miss them for you are not "present" when you are worried about yesterday or tomorrow.

We say to you again that everything in your life is in "Divine Order" just as God created it. Everything happens for a very good reason! There are no accidents. You are exactly where you are in perfect, divine timing. You, by your own thinking, bring on your life experiences. If you do not like your experiences,we say change your thinking. You do not realize your thinking and your belief system brings you experiences, as most of the time you don't want to take the responsibility. You would rather blame someone else for your predicaments.

Things move very slowly on the Earth plane so you do not always see the connection between your thought process and manifestation because you are impatient. You want what you want when you want it."

Q. What do I have to do to master patience?

"We say that manifestation of goals takes time on Earth. A lack of patience is really a lack of trust. We say, you have sowed many seeds, yet you do not wait for harvest time. You tug at the roots of the young plants, pulling them out of fertile soil and they whither and die. You have started many projects but you have given up somewhere between your first concept and the final completion. You came to the Earth to learn to trust your own ideas, to persevere, and to develop patience while doing so. It is a part of the curriculum on your planet.

We see by your despair you have blocked this creative flow by demanding outcomes before their time. We say, relax and know that God is at work. Trust His timing even though it may be different than yours. Reach to see the greater vision of the plan of Love and Light. Your plan does not see the greater picture. This is where we ask that you trust God's plan. He sees every aspect of it.

To help you see this clearly, imagine that the Earth is a classroom and is filled with opportunities for learning. You learn lessons and you graduate from those lessons. We say, you are on Earth for the experiences you're having, including learning patience. You never leave your spiritual path. There isn't a moment that isn't devoted to your learning. Remove the arrows from the target, aim and shoot again. No one is sitting in judgment of you. There is no punishment in archery - or in life! You are simply learning the virtue called patience.

We say that there are great rewards in the balance of mastering patience. All good comes to those who wait. Once you are aligned with God in your heart and mind, great opportunities are revealed to you. They are actually in front of you always, but we say if you focus on them and not on God, you will never see them and become more and more distraught with "impatience."

Find God first and you will have it all. We say your cherished goals are met when your head and heart are aligned in love. When you truly accept this, you will experience an exciting shift in consciousness and will be patient ever after.

Simply ask to see as God sees. In the moment you relax your trust in the Divine outworking of whatever you are anxious about, you will see them all resolved. Let your new guiding words be, "I let go and I see a miracle." Uncover your Light and let your radiance shine forth.

Remember, all thought creates and on Earth, creation moves very slowly. We say, be grateful for that! If every thought you had manifested instantly, you could be in deep trouble. The law is the same regardless of what kind of thought you're thinking. Whenever you have begun to change a thought, you will still experience the creations made from your past thinking due to the momentum from your previous thoughts. We call this growth and we say this is how you learn and grow on the physical Earth plane.

We assure you your changes will come, as they must come, for they will always reflect your thoughts and beliefs."

Q. I seem to go through life a lot faster than others do which makes me irritable. Am I pushing others too hard to speed up?

"The Earth plane offers many different speeds at which things get accomplished. Everyone moves at their own pace. Your pace is simply faster than most other's. But we ask you, what is speed anyway?

Let us open your thinking here. There is only now. It is illusion if you see varying rates of speed. It is judgment if you see one as being slower than yourself, or not doing what it is you say. If you seem to be going faster than someone else, it could be translated into you're pushing them too hard.

We suggest that call the Holy Spirit into your affairs, to guide you in dealing with others. Ask to be given the gift of knowing that all things happen in perfect, divine order, in God's timing, not yours.

Ask to be given this understanding so you may learn to relax and stop judging others so harshly. Then, we say, things will 'magically' fall into place. You will no longer resist time and schedules, speed or agendas. You will be given the knowledge of honoring others' schedules and it will no longer bother you if your pace doesn't match theirs."

Peace

"We are going to have peace even if we have to fight for it."
- Dwight D. Eisenhower

Q. Sreper, assuming that stress is at the root of disease and illness, how do you suggest we maintain a peaceful, healthy state even in the midst of calamity?

"We say unto you that in order to have peace and tranquility you must want to experience peace more than anything else. If you do not have peace in your world, we say unto you that there must be something else more valuable than peace that you hold dear.

Disease and suffering carry extreme importance in your world. Look at the money people make from those who are sick and heavy-hearted. Look at the attention the lonely people receive if they become ill. Sickness breeds attention from others while peace flows unnoticed. Peace is not very exciting.

We say to the conscious mind it seems that one would readily give up pain and agony for the peace of mind that God has promised you, but we see humans have placed much more value on illness and disease than on Peace and Love. We would fully embrace your decision to change to a peace-filled world. You see, it is our one and only duty to guide you away from pain and suffering and into the higher worlds of peace, beauty and grace where there is no turmoil and where all beings love one another equally.

You need to use your imaginations here, for there is nothing we can compare to this Love for you to truly grasp it. You already share God's Love for He has given His Love to all equally.

You who are in the flesh do not see this brotherly love and equality over your fears, which only aim to separate you and cut you off from this pipeline of Love to Source.

We say unto you, give up your fearful little dreams for they seek to keep you in hell. We ask you, when will you be willing to lift your sights toward Heaven and ask the angels to shine God's Light upon you, to deliver you on their gossamer wings to new heights and lift you from the muck and mire into a higher reality of peace where you truly belong? This is very easy to do and takes but your willingness to choose peace over what you have created.

Give peace a chance. Give God a chance. Forgive yourself and forgive God. Plant the seeds today and nurture peace as you would nurture a rose in your garden. To have peace you must practice peace. Give peace to yourself daily even if it is but a few minutes of quiet time, and give peace to your neighbor.

Practice, practice, practice peace! Ask to see only peace and you will see only peace. Set your sights higher than you ever have before and do not be lured from this new path, indeed, a higher road. Remember that peace is now your only goal.

We applaud you heartily, for now you stand beside us at Heaven's gate and your new world awaits you with warm welcome. We fling open the gate so that you never again struggle alone in darkness... unless you choose to experience aloneness and darkness.

We love you and invite you to be at peace in God's radiant Universe. Awaken from the deep sleep of the world you have known and open your eyes. Dawn has come and it is a bright new day. Arise and take a stand for peace. Do not be pulled off-course again.

We will guide you if you but ask for your angels to come to you. We love you more than you can know. Peace be with you.

Q. Are we really ready for world peace?

"As we see it from here, planet Earth is in a stage of upheaval. We see two distinct forces, one of peace wishers and one of those who still sleep. We say that peace shall prevail, but not without the element of human desire and effort of people everywhere joined as one in this desire. It is time now for every soul to decide for either peace or chaos.

Many souls incarnated wish for peace and are working for this end. They are indeed ready for peace. They live and move and have their being in love and contentment and peace is their reward. Those not yet fully awake shall soon join those already in the Light. They shall see the Light and choose to come to it.

We see many others who appear confused. The dawn is touching them, yet they do not know what this means. Our job is to send Light to them and hope they will choose to join with us. Others will choose to remain in their darkness where peace shall be impossible to them. They will not find it and will not hear its gentle knock upon their heart's door. To those souls we send the Light and Love of God to illuminate their path.

Are you ready for peace? Each and every soul must find the answer in their own heart because peace begins within the very depths of each and every soul. Those of you who desire peace must first become peaceful. Then peace can reach outward into the world as an expression of love and compassion from the heart.

We say unto you, be ready for peace by resolving your inner conflicts and you will see nothing but peace in your world. If you hold to one anger thought, you will see an angry world. The choice is yours to make. Remember, peace comes peacefully."

Prayer

Q. How does prayer affect us and change reality?

"Prayer is what brings to you the things you seek in life because prayer is the sacred place within where these things are given birth. It is prayer that manifests your dreams.

Your prayers are not just the sounds you say with folded hands on bended knee. Prayer is a compilation of all your thoughts and words. In order for you to change your reality, you must start with consciously directing your thoughts. And all prayers are answered!

As you begin to be consciously aware of every word you speak, be aware too that all of them create, even though it may seem to take time. The creation process moves slowly there, and most of the people do not have patience enough to see the connection between their words and their worldly reality. The question is, how determined are you? Are you absolutely ready for change? Be determined and set your mind to that path entirely and completely without a doubt. Pray over what it is you want to change and then release your prayer to the Holy Spirit."

A Prayer At Daybreak

Let this day be filled with Light
and bless us each and everyone
who passes through this door, this life.
Let me be willing to contribute
to the harmony of the planet,
to the life within this house.
Let me see only the highest good
no matter what my little self would rather see.
And let me touch someone's heart

exactly where I need to touch their heart
to lift them to a precious place within themselves.

Let me be willing to see only good
working in my life today
should I forget and wander from this goal,
to start the day with prayer,
to be willing to make any changes
to let go of what hurts me
even if I cannot see that it hurts me.

Bless my life with God's Love
and let me know it is God's Love
that guides me through the gateways
of my difficult moments,
through them to peaceful resolve
where only a blessing remains.

Let me remember that I have choices.
Let me see what You would have me choose,
and not let me slip into despair and confusion,
not for a second.
Rather, let me cling to Your Peace and never let go
of Your Goal of Love and Harmony
to fill my life this day and forevermore.

And, Dear God,
I ask to express my love fully
this bright and glorious day
and, when nighttime falls
let my heart be filled and overflowing
with even more love to give tomorrow.
Amen.

A Prayer at Twilight

As I let go of this day, and as nighttime falls,
let my heart keep the Light it saw
to know that I was able to extend peace and love
to those I met,
and to let only that become a part of
my memory tomorrow.

And, let me take this time right now
to erase all that is less than who I really am.
Let me not take into tomorrow that which is not
a part of me, or my goals.

Take from me my pain, my worries,
my petty grievances,
and allow me to be big enough to bless them
into nothingness now.
Let me awaken with a joyful heart and mind,
totally willing to see only good blessing my life
should I forget and wander from this goal.

Remind me to end the day with prayer
and joyful reflection.
Let me see that I was willing to make changes,
and I was able to let go of what hurts me.
Bless my life with Love
and let me know it is God's Love
guiding me through the gateways into the night.

Dear God, at the close of day,
as I close my eyes,
I see the deep blue night falling around me,
and across the planet,

quieting my mind of any troubles
I thought I saw today.

As I prepare to sleep,
I know I have been blessed,
my troubles are erased.
I release any shadow thoughts into the nighttime sky
where they disappear,
and when I open my eyes in the morning Light,
I will see that only a blessing remains.
Amen.

"We say, sometimes you are so conditioned and locked into your own "one-way street" of how you view life and the world around you that you don't realize the myriad of options available to choose from to change your life. During times of stress and emotional flare-ups, you react from old, familiar patterns which only lead you down the same old street again, right into desperation and despair.

We say to you, become a detective and see that wherever there is a problem, you will also see someone who is stuck, or who has been backed into a corner by his or her closed-mindedness. You need never again be trapped if only you would remember there are other streets to take, but have merely been blocked by your limited viewpoint.

Let us pray."

A Prayer for Openness

"Holy Spirit, help me so that I may take the blinders off and see the entire road map before me. Lead me beyond the appearances of the 'fences of limitation,' and lead me to greener pastures, pastures that nurture and support who I am now, in this moment, releasing me from all old goals that no longer serve my highest potential of good.

Give me new inspiration for creating my life experiences. Let me have the determination to replace pain with bliss in every step I take on this 'higher path.' I ask to be removed from limitation in my mind and heart, and I am willing to pull up the fences on all of my one-way mental streets that have lead me to the same sad destinations.

Today let me wake up. Fill me with the desire, God's desire through me, for a better life in which I am changed and renewed. And, let me not be afraid to change, but know that only good awaits to unfold to me now.

Dear God, open my eyes so I may see as you see. Let me know there are more ways than my way to see a situation. I realize that my mental focus determines the situations in my life and so let me wisely choose where I place my attention. Help me lift my focus from the things that trouble me to the solutions that would resolve them. Guide my internal sight to truly know what you would have me learn. Heaven help me let go of the pain and see only the blessing. Allow my heart to be open to hear a different answer than my own and let the new ideas wash over me, leaving me fresh and ready to create that which makes my heart sing. And let me know that the only thing I am stuck with is my own healing. Amen."

A Prayer to Heal the Heart

"I am willing to let go and let the angels speak their love through me. I relax and know I am a clear and open channel to receive the angel's thoughts, words and blessings into my life now. As I get my conscious mind out of the way, I relax and know the angel's love flows through me, heals me and teaches me to let go of anything that is not worthy of a child of God to carry. As I do this, my heart is healed and made whole. My mind willingly lets go of any unworthiness. Then, with their Golden Threads of Light, the angels mend my heart and blow their sparkling Light into it. Any dark thought is whisked away into nothingness where it is blessed and then disappears.

I am given this Love-Light to send to others whom I may have hurt. I know my angels can work their magic and will send their healing love and energy into their hearts and make them whole, if I but ask them and I do.

I release all guilt. I am not guilty. I am not responsible for someone else's life. I set others free. I am free to live my life as I wish, and I choose to blaze a trail of love wherever I go. I am not bound to anything less than what my heart desires. I am free and the world is a happier place. Thank you God and the messengers for God that this is so. Amen."

Procrastination

"You can't try to do things,
you simply *must* do them!" - Ray Bradbury

Q. How can I find the energy to break through this procrastination and get into doing the tasks I need to do, like straightening out the clutter in my house? What is blocking me?

"We say unto you to make the decision to do it, and then do it. Do you not see all the energy you are wasting in putting the chore off?

We can say to you from here there is much peace waiting for you in the balance. Make the decision to tackle your work and all things fall into place to support this decision. Look at how your choice to let things pile up supported you! We say it is the same law at work."

Prosperity Part One:
Financial Difficulties

"The highest reward for man's toil is not what he gets for it,
but what he becomes." - John Ruskin

Q. I am worried that I will not have any money to do the things I want to do. What can I do to let go of this idea?

"We say unto you, Dear Ones, there is abundance and wealth beyond your wildest dreams, however, you are more focused on either the money you have or the money you don't have. Money is a big issue because your values have been displaced by your ego, and what it says is important.

We would like to suggest you look at this in another way. The only item of real value is in remembering you are a child of a generous and loving Father. You are creation in its glory. Your glorious self remains intact even though you have walked through the veil of forgetfulness and do not remember. In fact we see that you hardly react to these words when we say them.

Let us remind you that you have been given the gift to co-create with the Creator and you are constantly creating the world you walk in. Therefore, we say call forth what is yours by Divine birthright and let the rest go."

Q. Sreper, we are disgusted over the fact that there are drug dealers making big money off of pushing drugs to children while Lightworkers, who are doing good work to raise consciousness, are not being supported financially.

"We say, the so-called "business of raising consciousness" is not about making riches, but in living a richer life. If the intention is for you to make a lot of money, then choose a business that makes a lot of money. Raising consciousness does not 'make money' as that is not its intention. As far as the drug dealers are concerned, there is more to the story than what meets your ego eyes. We say do not judge appearances. Rest assured that any so-called imbalance you see on the Earth plane is put into balance on a plane you don't see.

Earth school presents lessons to both the divine and those who still wail in darkness. You see both worlds and it is your choice which one you will live in and call home. Keep your noses clean and follow what is in your heart.

We will also add that there is a breath of fresh air regarding this on your Earth. Lightworkers are realizing their connection to their guardian angels who, when the angels are called upon, can and will help you align to your purpose of making a living. This is very important to know. Call on the angels! Put God first in your life and all your desires shall be added to your experience there."

Q. Why is it that so many people are having financial difficulties?

"Where you stand on the Earth today is likened to a fisherman standing in the midst of a fast-moving stream. Everything around you is changing very rapidly. Everything, that is, except your rigid attitudes. You do not allow the world to flow around you. You have grabbed on to a life preserver (a job or a career) many years ago, and have stayed in the same spot.

You need to live and go with the flow. We say, the way you have set up your society, it is nearly impossible for you to set yourself free. To retrain yourself in a new career would be expensive and time-consuming. We also say that this is a set-up from the ego and not how we would have it be. None of it.

So we answer you from your level in your current state of affairs. Life moves ahead, but you are still hanging on to yesterday's dreams. Loosen your fearful ego grip and allow yourself some space to dance. Let your old ideas of financial security go. Allow fresh ideas to flourish. Entertain the imagination – the ideas we send forth to you, for everything old shall pass away and no longer be useful in the world where you are headed.

There is great change upon the planet and we say it is going in the direction of the heart, away from the head. You are not on Earth to be a slave to a career that doesn't fulfill you or make you happy. Remember that *everything changes constantly*. Bet on nothing except change. We suggest you lighten up about that too, for the lighter you are, the more you will flow with life. We say, exercise those sea legs!"

Q. What can I do to make some money?

"It seems by your question that you are focused first on making money without much regard to what your heart's true desire is. The search outside of yourself will never bring you the peace and contentment you really seek.

We suggest you wear one hat at a time and choose carefully according to what is in your heart. Become the leader in your field of choice and let the monetary rewards come as a result of your reaching the goal. If, for example, your choice is to sell real estate, sell with the intent of helping your clients find their happy home, catering to them as you, yourself would love being catered to.

Too often greed is the goal. Many people are out to make quick cash and do not truly care about the welfare of those they serve. Although it seems enviable to be in a position of "having it all," do not be deceived by the glitter of ill-gotten gold. Your path is one of the heart. We say, seek the true gold that lies within you, and the outer gold shall come to you as well.

Know that it is the gold in the heart that you truly seek. Be not distracted by any lesser goals but work for, and out of love. We say you will be reaping the rewards of a happy heart later... and not too much later."

Q. I am worried over my divorce settlement and that my ex-husband will get everything we have. Help!

"We say, there is magic in release. Let go of your worries regarding 'who gets what,' for it is a barrier to receiving your Divine Inheritance from God. Once knowing this, why would you want to stand in the way? Let go of this concern and trust God. When have you ever been without before? As you let go of your concerns, watch as the universe answers an open heart. See what happens as your new attitude emerges, for your joy, your money, your good, in whatever form you call it, always comes to you according to your belief.

We suggest you release your old law that keeps you in fear of not having enough, because it is only a belief and it is what creates your not having enough. Bring your beliefs into into balance as to who you are today. Stop being hard on yourself. Loosen up the tight, limiting beliefs that no longer bring you the things you desire. You have our love and permission to do this, now give yourself these."

A Prayer for Releasing Limitations

"Create in me a new spirit, Father, and lead me to the still waters within my consciousness that I might know Your Truth that there is always plenty for everyone. What is mine shall come to me exactly when it is needed in my unfoldment to my highest good. I am well and I am wealth! God lovingly provides me with the entire world now. Remove my fears and my fences which limit God's Good from manifesting in my world. I release the past and forgive my limitedness. I open myself to receive God's good now, knowing in my heart the way is open unto me to follow. Let me get to work. Amen."

Q. It worries me that my finances fluctuate so much. Why does this happen?

"We say that one of the reasons you are on Earth is to learn that money continuously flows in and out of your life as the tides of the ocean crest and recede. If your finances are low, know that, in time, they will crest again. Then, a little bit later, they will recede again. Grow and recede, grow and recede and they will grow again. When you are in a "down time" in your financial state-of-affairs, keep in mind that, like the ocean, there will again be an increase. Ebb and flow.

We suggest you make it easy on yourself and learn to surf the waves of life. You will master this if you but realize that finances continually fluctuate. Rest knowing that there is little you can do to stop the waves rising and falling in the ocean, and there is little you can do to stop the financial waves from the same. But, we say, keep yourself balanced – as any good sailor must."

Prosperity Part Two:
Financial Abundance

"Whatever you do, or dream you can, begin it. Boldness has genius
and power and magic in it." -Johann Wolfgang von Goethe

Affirmation for Abundance

"Dear God, this day I go forward knowing there
is plenty. The universe gives me all that I need and
desire to be happy. I give myself all the love I can
express, knowing the Truth of Me, that I am the child
of a generous and loving Father. I let go of the worries that make me afraid I was forgotten. I am worthy of love and abundance. I gain more love and
self-esteem every moment of this day, and I choose
to share all that I am with those who are on my path
with me, for I know that in giving, I receive. I
emanate this Truth and my life is richly blessed. And
so it is."

"To create an experience of financial abundance, start
realizing the world is an abundant place. Your needs have
always been met. We are here to tell you that there is always
enough. With every breath you take, make this your new
affirmation and let go of the worry about lack. This shall
open the door to greater good! Worrying over lack only creates more lack for that is where your creative energy is
being spent.

We say, cease your worry over lack of financial abundance and instead, choose to bless all of your actions. Ask
for guidance in decisions. Look deep within your heart and
know that you always make inspired and sound investments. Bless your money and bless the avenues it travels.

See your money going through the world blessing everyone it touches, for you are one of those who will receive from your giving. You are the giver and you are also the recipient. Whatever thoughts you send into the Universe are what you will continually create and experience.

We suggest you send only blessings. Send only love and you shall see nothing but love returned to you."

Q. How can I achieve financial security? How can I stop creating self-sabotaging behavior?

"We see financial security will be flowing to you as a result of changing to a new self-winning attitude. The change must first occur on the mental level. Choose to bless your financial decisions instead of worrying over them. Know in your heart you always make sound judgments and inspired investments. Bless your money and bless the avenues it travels. Bless those who are benefited for you are one of those who receive from your own giving."

Q. Sreper, why is it that those who work for the Light and for the good of all seem to be struggling financially? How can 'Lightworkers' make a living when it appears they are not being supported by the higher realms they work for?

"Oh, but they are supported by the higher realms! Where are you placing your goals? You must realize that personal goals and ambitions vary for different people. It may not be the goal of a Lightworker to make a living from performing spiritual work. Mother Teresa would be an example of this.

We see this is really a question about setting and attaining personal goals, and caution you to not judge what others are doing as you're tempted to do when viewing life through the ego's eyes. The ego only sees a tiny part of the picture and then judges it. Keep in mind that there are many souls on Earth who do not have the goals of making money. Be careful to keep your judgment out of this, for it will only serve to pull you off your own yellow brick road.

Let us re-phrase the question... 'Why is it that some people are financially successful while others are not?' Notice we disregard any reference to what a person's profession is and look to the intent they hold in their heart. Some people's goals are solely aligned with making money while others are not.

What anyone manifests, or does not manifest, is a reflection of their prevailing belief system. If you are not financially successful, it is because you are not focused on being financially successful. Somewhere inside of you, you're distracted from a goal of having financial abundance.

Belief systems run deep within your individual consciousness. You are also influenced by Earth's collective consciousness, which may be subtle within you, but plays a huge role in your lives. To get to the root of a belief in lack, you must do some digging and clearing. Most individuals are not aware of the core beliefs they carry around and unknowingly perpetuate because the foundation thought did not originate in their own mind. They have taken on a belief in lack from someone else, perhaps inheriting their parents' poverty consciousness.

Where these thoughts originate is not the issue, but weeding them out of your consciousness is. That is, of course, if you're making a new goal of having success and prosperity. Then, if that is true, be clear about this and work toward it and let nothing distract you! We say it is very important to release any guilt you may have over the right to have this new life, and have it abundantly. You are not on Earth to suffer in any way. Your suffering is an illusion which is made by you and is also dispelled by you.

It is easier to for you humans to believe in lack rather than in abundance, for lack is the predominant thought-form on your plane and at the present time, it carries the most creative energy. To dwell among this negativity is still the path of least resistance, for it takes courage to stand up against the prevailing wind and take the brunt of the assault from that action.

To change this trend will take conscious effort and practice. But if your wish is financial success, we say you must weed out all the negative thought-forms you hold regarding earning and having money. Dig deep into the Earth of your subconscious mind and turn up the roots of these poverty patterns and pull them out. Be diligent to this effort and you will succeed, for you must succeed even as you succeeded at creating lack.

Your truest intention is what will always manifest. Ask for new and prosperous thinking to come to your mind and align with your heart. Ask to be shown the steps you need to take to achieve your new goals. Remember, no one holds you in poverty but you. You hold yourself there by your beliefs. If you want to create more financial abundance in your life, then you must first open yourself to it. Give yourself the permission to have abundance and accept the outpouring of Grace into your life now. Align yourselves with the highest goal you can possibly imagine and clear the way for it to come to you. Stop the incessant judging of others and what they have created for their goals.

There is ample supply for everyone. Dismiss all greed and envy from within your hearts and keep your eyes on the prize, for the truth is that whatever you hold dear in your heart also comes into your life."

Quit Smoking

Consult not your fears but your hopes and your dreams.
Think not about your frustrations, but about your unfulfilled potential.
Concern yourself not with what you tried and failed in,
but with what is still possible for you to do." - Pope John XXIII"

Q. I have tried several methods but I haven't been able to quit smoking. What is sabotaging my desire and efforts to quit smoking?

"We ask you, 'Have you given yourself permission to quit? Have you said to yourself that you truly desire being a non-smoker?' Whatever is written across your heart is what shall manifest. We see that you think you wanted to quit, but you haven't really wanted to give it up yet. When you truly desire to leave smoking behind you, you will quit, and there will be no more talk about it. What desire do you wish more? This is what is manifesting.

This is a smoke-screen of sorts too. You have wanted to be in Earth to reach beyond the physical senses and to know there is greater meaning behind all things. Your ego self has been afraid of what is behind the screen, and your body has manifested a desire to smoke to block this sight. Perhaps you have felt a little tension in your stomach area, an empowerment you are feeling, but it yet surprises you because it is new to you. You have never experienced such a thing as trust in your self at this new level.

Follow your heart on this. It is time for you to turn inward and find yourself."

Relationships

" Sing and dance together and be joyous, but let each one of you be alone, even as the strings of a lute are alone, though they quiver with the same music." - Kahlil Gibran

Q. Sreper, what is the purpose of relationships?

"We see that many of you in Earth ponder relationship dilemmas and it seems that no matter how hard it is for you to love another and get along well with them, there always seems to be trouble and pain. We seek to give you a clearer understanding so that you may learn to truly love someone in your lifetime there. We dare say unto you that love's rewards far outweigh the pain you suffer in finding it, for once your heart has truly experienced love, it shall never settle for less than that. Not ever.

Earth school was set up for you to learn and experience all matters of the heart. You see, not just love exists on that plane. It was set up for you to also know love's opposites, that by your free will you might choose love once having seen the difference. So, dear ones, when you are in deep despair, feeling as though love has passed you by, we ask for you to think again and remember what we have come to tell you this day. All that you learn in Earth school is not in vain. There is a wealth of experience and information your heart learns and sends back to its Source.

We ask you to know that whatever pain you have suffered, although you may not understand this, it is all for good reason. We say unto you, your soul's purpose is to learn the matters of the heart."

Q. What was originally intended regarding relationships? What is to be shared and learned from them?

"What we observe at this time is that there is great

dependence upon one another at this time. It appears to us that humanity has lost one of its basic instincts, its ability to love and honor Self, for if you truly loved and honored yourselves, you could not help but to love all your human brothers and sisters. If you are involved with one who we term to be 'dependent,' we can actually see your energy being drained from you.

We envision this: Be in love completely in the moment in which you stand. Think not about tomorrow or the days gone by. Be still and feel your love now. Know this feeling well. Know this to be the Source from where you get your strength to live. Learn this well for it is why you are on the Earth.

To be complete, and to complete the cycle, as it were, as you receive this love from Source, you must also express your love by giving as you receive. You hold in your minds the notion that love must be shared with someone who travels with you, alongside you, one who is there for you, perhaps forever. To this we have good news and we have some surprises, Dear Ones. Give and share your love freely as the wind that blows through the trees - strong, sure of itself, and free. See this as the love between two people. It too shall be strong, sure of itself, and free. Do not try to own it or control the way it goes. Let it be and let it freely exist with you. Let go every single notion you have that you must somehow bottle this wind and store it up as though there will be no more wind tomorrow.

Do not be afraid love will run out and you will be left without it. If you knew how much love exists in your world and could come into your life if it were but welcomed, you would laugh at your tiny thought of seeking to capture control over it!

So, we come to you this day to tell you to claim your

freedom and allow the force of love to sweep through you fully. Breathe it in as you would the breeze on a spring day; cool, sweet, refreshing. Know it is renewing you from head to toe, beyond this plane on the unseen realms it is renewing all of you.

Become aware of your feelings and stay on top of them, for they give you great messages which are the answers you seek regarding your personal relationships. At the very first sign of disharmony, of your attempts to control the wind, we suggest you examine that feeling and look for options. See what adjustments could be made to realign yourself and either make those adjustments, or let it go in that moment. Don't wait. Waiting is also a form of control. Remember, love flows freely to you. Take your fear out of it. Don't cling to hurts and disappointments. Make any adjustments early and don't get caught up in playing games of control. From here it looks just as silly as chasing the wind!

We give you the picture of two buoys on the water, happily bouncing to and fro as the wind and the waves move them. Suddenly, one buoy is snagged up by the other and can no longer bob freely. This is the caution sign to look for.

Ask yourself what are you trying to control in the other person that made the happiness and freedom stop? What is he or she trying to control in you that made the happiness and freedom stop? These are valuable clues to determine when a relationship has instead become a game of control. May you begin this day to love freely, and the starting point is to love yourself as we love you."

Q. Sreper, what keeps us bound to old relationships when we know they are not healthy and no longer serve us?

"Fear. Fear of what may lie ahead for you to experience and/or a fear of believing that what is, is all there is. You tend to limit yourselves. The human race fails to see into the future for it is 'unknown' and therefore is 'fearful.' Humanity has a habit of that which is not understood or accepted in your reality, is therefore, something to be feared."

Q. How would one know when a relationship is no longer healthy?

"We say to become fully conscious of your own self, ask, and then in all honesty, answer yourself. Ask if you are fulfilled mentally, spiritually, emotionally and physically? Is your mind creating that which is good? Is your spirit oozing with joy? Does your body sing notes you didn't know you had? Then, we say that the relationship serves you well, for it brings joy into your heart.

The earth plane is filled with much sadness for there are far too many humans who have agreed within themselves to settle for less than what they truly could have and experience on that plane. Somewhere in time you have lost your passion to create that which you love and that which your Father has given you as your birth right. You have instead chosen to back away from His gifts and have closed the gates to Heaven believing yourselves unworthy to be in the kingdom. You have settled for less than the best and therefore you live with fear instead of joy and bliss, unconditional love could give you.

We ask of you, to reach higher now. Raise your personal standards of love and increase your capacities for love, and walk joyfully through the gates. Indeed, we say open wide your hearts and know yourselves as individual expressions of God but have simply forgotten.

Reach within your hearts and pull the glory of your own Light out and let this Light shine brightly unhindered, allowing it to fill every cell of your being, for the time is now that your prayers and wishes all be fulfilled. This is the glorious time that your hearts have waited for and so we say to reach within, and find that which is ready to burst forth with song, and fear not, for the melody is one you remember from long ago. Let your future days be filled with the activity of letting go of fear and release all negative ideas from yourselves (your cells). In so doing, you allow the new, yet ancient Light to enter. This will nurture the promises of yesterday and water the seeds of Love your soul planted within you long ago.

We also wish for you to note that you have never made a mistake in your comings and goings, nor have you erred in your personal relationships. You only think you have and we say to release these ideas. Remember that everything that happens on Earth is a learning experience and need never be judged beyond that. You enter into a relationship when it feels right and you leave a relationship when it feels right. There are no failed relationships except those that fail to teach the lesson. All things happen in their due season, and we say let each moment arrive to bring forth its own sweet gift. Linger not on sweetness that is past for you shall lose sight of today's precious offerings.

Be prepared to receive the gifts each new moment opens to you. Do not be 'hung up on' what has occurred in the past or what will occur in the future. Keep yourselves free in each moment to choose what feels right in your heart. Rekindle the passion you came into Earth with and let that be your guide on that plane.

We say unto you, Dear Ones, allow yourselves to experience your individual freedom from the bondage fear would seek to keep you in. Recognize this tendency and advance to the Light. You need not suffer with anything less than good ever again if you are but willing to just let it go!

Call on us and we are there to guide you. You never need to slay the dark dragons alone. We ask that you be blessed with Love and Light from the highest heavens."

Q. Sreper, in our relationships with others we sometimes find we're caught in the middle of a situation that in the end turns out to be another person's lesson with no apparent lesson for us. Often we are victims because of our position or feelings we have for the other person in the relationship, i.e., husband to wife, parent to child, boss to subordinate. Why are we allowed to be victimized in such painful ways if the major crisis/lesson is for another person?

"We say to you that this is one of your greatest lessons in truly loving and trusting that love. You are in these situations to learn to listen to your heart. You must turn down the volume of your screaming ego voice in all matters, especially those concerning others in your closest of relationships. These are the most difficult lessons for you to learn because of your ego-attachment to the situation, or to the other person.

You think that to love another human being means to be involved with their emotional being, to make their curriculum your own. One of the greatest lessons you are presented to learn on the Earth plane concerns letting go of these attachments and to still love the other person without conditions, no matter what. Regardless if they are learning their lesson or not, your role has always been to send them pure love, without any conditions on your love.

This is where it gets tricky because you have always complicated the simple task of giving love with the ego fear of losing what it "loves." This fear actually fuels the control dramas to play themselves out and to hang on to the object of its so-called love.

Do not be fooled. There is always something in these situations to learn. Your lesson is to discern real Love from ego fears. Most often these are confused, but if you take time to contemplate the situation before diving in heart first, you will be able to sort out the ego whims from what is really real. You are not without help in the discerning process. You have the skills and guidance of your guardian angels.

Remember to call on us and you will not face these heart-wrenching lessons alone. Once you have successfully gone through the middle of these lessons, they become easier. Do not hold any fear regarding that these lessons will be painful, but instead allow yourself the open-mindedness and willingness to walk the way of the heart. Leave behind the littleness of the ego in yesterday."

Q. I keep attracting crummy relationships and would like to know what to do to have a lasting, healthy, loving relationship?

"We say, you shall stop attracting these "less than good" relationships when you are feeling good about yourself. You are already perfect in your Creator's eyes. You were never anything less than that. But your mind is a mirror to the world as you choose to see it.

If you don't like the movie you are watching, you need to change the film in the projector. We say, first change your view to loving and accepting yourself completely. Then, see what type of people you attract to your world."

Q. I can hardly stand to work in my office because of negative co-workers who are always in competition with each other. Short of finding another job, what can I do to heal this situation and restore my workplace to harmony?

"We say unto you, often these types of situations stem

from something left unresolved from a past-life that has come to you again for you to heal now. Radiate love to those around you and love is what will be radiated back to you. If you send judgment out to those you work with, judgment is what you will get back.

In your daily prayers send brilliant love to those you work with. If they cannot tolerate the love radiated throughout the office, if they cannot hold that vibration, they will leave and seek a job elsewhere that supports their lower vibration. The only thing necessary for you to do is release your mental hold on how this plan will unfold.

Also, release the thought that the workplace is 'competitive.' We ask you to open wide to its beauty and rest with the new knowledge that you need not compete in order to win God's favor, for you already have it as your Divine birthright. Release your struggle with this co-worker and ask to see the blessing in it instead.

Allow yourself to be at peace. See the shining face of love within everyone you meet and you will see nothing but love returned. This lesson carries the peace you have sought forever. May it bless you now."

"Dear Ones, we see the pain in human hearts that relationships cause, and we say there exists a universal lesson to learn love and to set your hearts free. It is about learning to trust your deepest feelings and to know at the deepest levels what true love is. We bait the trap, so to speak, with human beings to whom you are attracted and for whom you have an affinity. What better way to get your attention then through such heart strings?

The reason for emotional tugs is that you are being lifted into knowing new levels of love which are now opening within your heart. You need to open these doors and free yourself to experience this new and expanded love. You are being asked to bury the past and bury the hatchet. The old ways of relating and patterns of behavior no longer serve you and no longer compliment your energy. They need to be discarded before entering the gateway where you are going.

Cleanse yourself and be free from all psychic dirt left-over that dulls your shiny brightness that remains from the emotional tug-of-war. Create in yourself a bright, clean heart and be ready for the higher levels of love to be expressed in and through you. Love will be back once you are shining brightly again, for your Light is what is attractive to others.

Get busy developing yourself. Do the work you are here to do. See your heart refreshed and see yourself as a shining star leaving a glowing warmth in whatever you touch and in whatever touches you. It will be very attractive and love will return when the coast is clear again.

Bless and release yourself from all old ties. Be that which you want in order to attract that which you want. Whiny begets whiny. Goddess begets God."

A Prayer To Heal Relationships

"Dear Angel of Mine, help me to see as God sees. Give me the eyes to look upon this relationship as God would, knowing that it comes as a gift to lift me and them to a fuller understanding, to a richer experience of life. Even though my little self cannot understand why this relationship is so, my Higher Self is learning that this is Love's way of working out the details so all of the people involved in this will benefit in the highest way possible for them.

Heaven help me remember that all things work together for the good of all concerned, and there are no accidents in the unfolding of higher consciousness. I ask to be set free of any worry and fret I carry over this, knowing I am learning the valuable virtue called Trust. I do not understand my involvement in this, but God does and I allow His Wisdom to flow freely into my heart and theirs, knowing fully that His Golden Rays of Love heal them and me now.

I also ask the angels to be quick to alert me next time should I fall back into my lazy habit of worry and ask they help me let go and see God's healing Love in action before I get a chance to involve or hurt myself again. Amen."

Q. Sreper, what does one do after breaking off a long term relationship and he or she is afraid to love again? How long does a person need to go on searching, to find himself after suffering a loss? What is unconditional love anyway?

"We come to light the way for your hearts are yet shrouded in darkness. First, we say drop the words 'unconditional love' for that implies there are conditions!

Your ears are listening to patterns taught you in the past. You must learn to live and love in each and every moment and to let go of your old self. Let it disappear into the nothingness of the past. Unless you forgive - which really means to let go of the past, you will surely repeat it.

The lesson you are facing is to let go of the need for painful realities to be your teacher and to live through the eyes of love right now. Love relationships can end in peace! Change your thoughts regarding the outcome you want to see. Let your hearts be open to peaceful resolution. Love yourself, and extend only love to your ex-lovers no matter what has happened. Perhaps, at another time, you were their way-shower on a path to a brighter reality. If you choose to stay in unforgiveness, you shall never discover love or fulfill the reason why you came to Earth. Stop hiding under the rocks of fear. We give you the strength to rise above that density and live! Remember, you live only to discover Love. We say, do not afraid of it. Learning love is why you reside on Earth. If you fail in this, we dare say that you shall not live at all.

Let go of the need for pain to be your teacher. Let Love light your way. We see that it is the soul's desire to experience love. Your heart center calls to be opened and set free, to be listened to, and to be trusted. It is the soul's reason to be in Earth life, to experience the physical realm, for there is no other place in creation where love can be learned.

The mission of the people in Earth is to know what love is; by feeling it and then by extending it to the rest of creation, even if it be given to one person at a time. This is the human mission. We see that this is a difficult thing for you to do. Some seem to be so far removed from love that they are lost, but their heart remembers and it is still their desire to find it. All things in Earth are motivated by love. Behind anger and hatred, their is a voice calling for love. Some do not yet know that to seek and find love, they need only look to the multi-dimensional vastness within their own heart, to their own Self, and see the love there shining. Too many people look for someone on the exterior to love them and then, and only then do they feel it must be okay to love themselves. This is not the way love works and is the cause of misery for many.

Today we ask that you know that you are Love, and you are already loved. The power of love is so great, it can literally move mountains! This power is within all of Creation to use. The problem is, everyone loses their way, either they are afraid of, or are in denial of wanting or needing love.

We say to you, come home, people! Come home to your heart. You are on Earth to discover what is in your heart, and the way is through the heart. You are there to master your feelings and emotions – to love and be loved – and to stop giving your power away to your head, or ego.

To every human quest, the answer is always love. If you do not know what to do, listen to your heart. It knows the steps you need to take. It is time now for you to follow your bliss and let go of all past miseries your head has taught you for this is the source of unhappiness.

We dare say... risk loving again, for it is why you walk upon the Earth. It is time for you to put down your defenses, get out from under the rocks of fear, and harmonize with the song written in your heart."

A Prayer to Heal Conflicts

"Dear God, as we go through this storm, through the very eye of it, at times passing through the wind and high seas, let us know we will get back to center and back to peace, for the Universe is based on balance. For a while we give and for a while we receive, until it is time to give again. Love leads the way, for it is the path of the heart and it beckons us.

We have followed as faithful children follow the call of their parents. In our love we come together, to be together to express the love that has been given us. Let this day be the beginning of an even greater love than we have ever known!

I ask, Dear God, for the Wisdom to accept this Love and the responsibility for it. Teach me how to express it and use it to make us happy. I ask that both our hearts be restored and that we have the

courage to endure whatever our Love asks of us –
forgiving everything in its path, for we never intend
to inflict hurt upon each other.

Dear God, I ask that our hearts be healed now
and that your peace prevails in every relationship.
Let our Lights shine brightly in us – radiant and
alive – blessing us everywhere. And, Dear God I ask
that we both be willing to see our love and nothing
else between us. Amen."

Retirement

"Happiness is not a state to arrive at,
but a manner of traveling." -Unknown

Q. I was given an early retirement. This lifestyle change in my mid-fifties is frightening. What advise can you give me?

"Retirement does not mean it is the end of life or that you are finished. All you have done is end a work relationship that was no longer fruitful to your spirit. It no longer served your highest purpose. Your higher self knows this and that is why you left the ego's comfort zone. Your physical self cannot see the bigger picture, nor can it understand the total dynamics of retirement. Your ego self is somewhat panicky and needs to get used to not having its safety net of a nine-to-five activity.

We ask you to give yourself permission, as it were, to lift yourself above the veil of tears you find yourself drowning in, for things aren't as bad as they seem. Look again and see the glory of your life. Instead of choosing to see sadness over what has been or what could have been, look straight ahead to see the beauty and the Light coming upon you. You have much more to accomplish there than you know. You have merely completed a chapter in your life, not the entire book.

It's been a long haul and you are resting at a wayside. You are rechecking your map to see which road to take. See this as merely a time-out, and remove all unnecessary pressures from yourself. Gather your energy and plan your new route. Give yourself credit for where you have been and look to the place you want to go, for this is all part of the Divine Plan."

Self Esteem

"No one can make you inferior without your consent." -Unknown

Q. Sreper, why don't I feel 'whole, perfect, and complete' even though my angels have told that I am. How can I adopt this new attitude and feel this perfection all the time?

"We see in your darkness that your journey has been long and has taken you far away from the Light of Who you are, into the depths of creation in your lower Earth worlds. This is not to say that this route you have taken is 'bad,' or 'wrong,' for we do not judge it, but it is to say that you have been steeped within the dimensions of Earth for eons of time, as you know time to be, and have indeed forgotten your way home.

You have forgotten your Creator and you have forgotten your brother who walks beside you. You've been looking for that which seems to be 'missing,' and while all of that world appears very real to you, we say unto you – with full strength of these words – that it is not your True Reality! It only seems so because your minds and your egos have made you believe it is so.

We say, let go of all your judgments. We have come at this late time on your Earth, to awaken you and help you step from your beds. We have come to take your hands and lift you from your veritable 'sea of slumber' that you have found yourselves in. You stand on the threshold of a grand new beginning.

All of you have chosen to be where you are to fulfill your promise to everything that exists in Creation with you, and beyond those walls – to wake up and smell the roses of True Reality, and to clearly see that which is really real, instead of your substituted dreams for it."

Q. How can I heal my inferiority complex?

"Why do you let your Light be diminished so? This shall never bring you peace. You may answer us by saying you are shy, and you feel you must "bow down" to those who are around you, letting their lights shine brighter than yours. You feel rather inferior to those around you, thinking their Light is always greater and more beautiful than yours.

We say nonsense! You must begin to appreciate the gift of Light which the Creator says is *you!* This Light is the essence which is you. It is your soul. We see that you have buried yourself as one would cover a lamp under a lamp shade... the Light still shines, but is shrouded in darkness.

We say you came to the Earth to experience Earth's Light. You came to experiment, to see how things felt to you, and to play and have fun learning about love. But long ago, since your arrival, you backed off from this Love-Light idea and became ashamed of your feelings.

We tried to reach you but our voices were not loud enough to be heard over the clamor in your own head saying you were sinful and should be condemned for things you experimented with in Earth.

Now, that we have your attention we say that this is a great day to celebrate! Listen not to the voices of the world for you are not of that world. You are there to have your love be awakened and expressed. Be neither shy nor ashamed of it. Stand tall. There is enough love in your heart to share with many people and many people will come into your world seeking this from you. We say, "Be still and know *you* are God." Act as God would act in human clothing, that is, not in bondage of humanness. Clothe yourself in glory. Unwrap yourself from this humanness, for it seeks to drag you down. It is simply a role you chose to play for this act in the drama you are appearing in. Know that this is coordinated for your learning and shall but disappear into the Light of Lights when the lesson is completed."

Q. What can I do to heal my sore mouth?

"We say, the soreness in your mouth is stemming from low self worth, from putting yourself down, and not believing in yourself. Your words have been speaking false about you and have festered themselves here. You would not treat a new-born baby like you have treated yourself, and you are as a new-born on this path of yours.

We see you becoming brighter and lighter as you learn to honor yourself in new ways. Be who you are. Realize you are a beloved Child of God and go forth positively into your days. The Light you shine will fall upon those whose eyes are ready to see. Positively express the love you are. Your insecurities will fall away and you will feel in your heart the love that surrounds you.

We need to say that life lessons mount up, as it were, if the soul's purpose has been ignored or postponed. We do not come so that you can beat upon yourself for not doing things differently. We come to tell you the sweetest, brightest news and that is you can begin again, right here and now.

Do you know that God is not complete without you? If all souls were to suddenly return to Heaven except you, there would be no Heaven. Heaven would wait for your return in order to be complete.

Therefore, we say with full confidence that the world awaits you. Join with it now. Your past hurts and disappointments can be wiped away, and indeed already have been except in your own mind where you entertain them still. We say to you, let go of what hurts you. This is a new day and a new beginning. Take up the new life being offered to you and forgive the past."

An Affirmation to Heal Self Image

"Daily, stand with your arms open wide as though you were reaching to embrace the sun, for in truth you are! Look upward toward the sky and say, "I accept my Divine Heritage as a Dearly Beloved Child of the Universe (of God the Father, Creator, Goddess, Mother Earth) now. I stand ready to walk the higher path to God. His Will radiates throughout my life and I shine with His Glory. So be it."

Sexual Abuse

""Our biggest hurdles can also be
our biggest miracles" - Rev. Nancy Freier

Q. Will you comment on my sexual abuse experience as a child? What can be done to heal this now?

"We see that you entered this life feeling like you were a victim needing persecution. Being in such a consciousness, you attracted those who needed to abuse someone. Consciousness attracts the same consciousness. This, as in all things, can be healed through forgiveness, providing one has the desire to forgive. If there is no desire to forgive, ask the Holy Spirit for it to be instilled in you.

The Lord said to forgive those who harm you, forgive those who persecute you. Forgive them for they know not what they do. We ask you, why would you want less than what God would give you?

Consciousness changes constantly. You have the power to change through the practice of forgiveness. You can actually rewrite your history! You can be who you want to be today, and through faith, move into bliss tomorrow.

Practice loving yourself and being patient with yourself while you are learning. Would you discipline a toddler for not knowing, say, how to solve an algebra problem? There is no hurry for this learning except in the ego-mind which created time and hurry. These things you have come to Earth to learn. Forgive and let go, trusting that all things are working together in perfect, Divine Order."

Sickness and Trauma: Stopping the Cycle

"Often the test of courage is not to die but to live." - Vittorio Alfieri

Q. Sreper, why is it that some people seem to be sick all the time while others never get sick? If they're not physically sick, they seem to always be in some kind of trauma?

"People are at different levels of enlightenment which means that their level of creating their reality will vary too. Those who are at a low level will thrive in creating illness and trauma. We say these people also show a need for attention from others – in whatever way they can attain it. From their childhood experiences, many have learned they can get attention and love from their parents or caregivers by creating sickness. As they grew up, they continued to use illness to get attention.

Look back on your life and notice the times when you were ill. In your assessment, ask yourself whose attention were you seeking. Why? What was happening in your life at the time you were ill? If you track this, you will see the reasons why you became ill, or had that accident when you did. If you are willing to be completely honest with yourself, you will learn some valuable information about how and why you create what you do. Turning up this evidence could be more valuable than us giving you the information from here.

Many of you still create illness for attention and love from others simply because you aren't aware that you can rise above that ego drama and create from a much higher place, and attract more radiance and Light into your life. That is precisely what we are here to help you do.

We stand by watching your life on Earth unfold in ways

that bring pain to you. Then, when you invite us in, we rush in with the answer, but it goes unheard, it seems, until you have had enough pain. Only then do your ears open wide to listen to another way. And there is another way.

We say to you, become willing to hear the call. Ask to be released from the cycle you have grown so accustomed to in your thinking and creating and let it go. Stop judging what has always been and what will always be, and see new possibilities you. We ask you to see that they are all possible no matter what you have created in the past. You can begin to create a healthy, happy life starting right now if you are but willing. Let your past fully dissolve.

Step up to the Light! Ask your angels to guide you as you walk a new path. Be willing to let go the need for negative attention from others knowing that what you really want is love at the highest level. Wanting this, cancels out the other. Wanting this, you will settle for nothing less than perfect health. Wanting this, you will see the shifts take place in your inner consciousness and as these shifts happen, your life will change and you will no longer need or want negative attention again. It drags you down!

Now, you will open to a much higher path, a step at a time. Do not lose sight of this new goal as changes in consciousness take a little time on your plane to manifest, but they will happen given the power of intention from your heart and mind. We say you must want this Light more than what you have known before and so shall it become real to you. Ask and it will happen. We ask you, are you ready to be well and happy?"

Q. Sreper, are there words to say that will cause us to have a shift in consciousness? Would you supply us with an affirmation or a meditation?

"Yes, of course. As with most things, words are like a catalyst for you. They can open the way for change to begin and new life to flourish, both within you and in your outer world. As we have said, first comes the willingness to open to something new. Next, say new words to create a new mind set. Then, new life shall follow.

Here are some new words for you to begin with. If possible, give yourself at least a half an hour a day, preferably upon waking, to encourage this new habit. If a half hour is not possible in the morning, do 15 minutes in the morning and another 15 minutes in the evening, as you end your day and go back into sleep. Use your sleep state to help you create that which you desire because it is a most creative time.

Start this time period with the following words"

A Prayer to Shift Consciousness

"Dear God, I ask to be lifted to a higher state of consciousness to see as you see. Spiritualize my intellect and let me loosen the grip physical reality has on my mind and heart. Let my experience be expansive... let me see as you see. Give me the inner strength to achieve this goal knowing that nothing else could be more important.

Dear God, let my life be changed from this shift in consciousness... this new way to view life. Let my life be a blessing to myself and may I leave a legacy that blesses someone else. Amen."

"May you be blessed with the ability to see as God sees. Indeed, may the highest possible vision always prevail and keep you from hurting yourself."

Soul Purpose

"Happiness, that grand mistress of the ceremonies
in the dance of life, impels us through all its mazes and meanderings,
but leads none of us by the same route." - Charles Caleb Colton

Q. What is my soul's purpose in this lifetime?

"Your soul's purpose is to take in all the joys that it can for the purpose of nourishing itself. Nature is the way in which one truly receives comfort in the Earth plane. Being immersed in nature is the closest remembrance of 'home' or what the Christian calls 'Heaven.'

Indeed, we see that your soul would be nourished fully by making this choice to your physical being into nature, in whatever way that feels right to you, wherever that may be... the snow-capped mountains or the sunny beaches, you shall be restless and searching for your 'divine connection' elsewhere – in your relationships and in your livelihood. But the question will always remain in you, tugging at you until you hear its call and rest in nature. Once this is fulfilled, it will be expressed through your relationships and livelihood.

We say to you, follow what your heart is telling you today and get into the natural flow of the Earth's rhythm within you. Let it pulsate and radiate throughout your being. Express yourself through nature by immersing yourself in it. By that we suggest working in it, even if that means planting a single tree right now.

Speak to this tree and let it speak to you. Great secrets will be revealed to you this way. Indeed, we say that great work awaits you, our Dear Child of Light. It is your heart's song now for you to sit up and pay attention to it."

Q. Which school would be the most helpful to me on my

spiritual journey? Is there a teacher or organization you would recommend?

"We dare say you are afraid to make some steps in fear that you take the wrong one. We say to you that you cannot make a mistake. But we also make note that you have a misplaced desire. We see in your heart that it is more a need to belong to an organization than it is for what the organization teaches you. This is what has you caught up in a whirlwind and you simply need to become clear on the direction you truly want to take.

We ask you, is it not all right with you to study many things that interest you without having to sign your very soul over to one of them? Is it not okay with you to be involved or interested in more than one line of thought at a time? Is it not okay to explore new avenues without a lifelong commitment to just one of them? Is it not okay to do one thing, and later if you so choose differently, to allow yourself to do something else again?

You need not sign yourself over forever to one thing, but rather we suggest that you start to allow yourself to flow with what is in the moment now. Do not look too far ahead of where you are, for it is the giant steps that scare you. Allow yourself to take the smaller steps that will lead you to gain the greater wisdom that comes as a result of these steps you take now. In other words, cross the bridge when you get to it and not before.

You are a wondrous being who is so much more than you have yet realized and are on the Earth now exploring what third-dimensional Earth School is teaching. We say go ahead and learn all that you are attracted to learning and don't get too hung up on traditions. You're there to break through these barriers, not to uphold them! Forget the limits and reach further than that.

Use the tools that are available to bring you to the stepping-off point where your soul needs you to be. You are a leader, not a follower.

We say, listen to that still, small voice within you which is your heart's voice for all your answers now. Be not alarmed at the changes about to occur for you. You are ready to take these chances now and they are all guided. In time you will discover that Truth lies within you. There are no more boundaries of separation. Break through them now, indeed break them all! Open the doors for others to follow in your footprints. This is why you came to Earth."

A Prayer to Know My Soul's Purpose

"Dear Heavenly Father, the Great Spirit Who resides in me and in all things, help me have the faith I need in order to know you also reside in my brothers and sisters; to know that you are guiding us to our goals of complete soul fulfillment. It is not mine to know your ways of how this will happen and therefore, I ask to be free of being responsible for them.

I am not my brother's keeper, but ask for Light, knowledge and strength be given each and every sibling so they may find their own soul's purpose. I ask to be of service wherever and whenever I can be for helping them on the road to discovering their highest good, but keep me off the highway so that I do not block what needs to come to them.

All things happen for very good reason regardless of the circumstance. Keep me from placing judgment on anyone, but teach me to bless and release them into Your good hands. I realize that in so doing, I free myself.

I walk forward in the Light and no longer stand in anyone's shadow. Dear God, I am filled with Your Light and Vision, and I now go about my business of accomplishing my life's work. Amen."

Spirituality

"Every day people are straying away from the church
and going back to God." - Lenny Bruce

Q. Sreper, what is spirituality? People seem to confuse it with religion?

"Spirituality defines the act of revering one's own spirit to guide them through life in physical matter. It is what we like to call 'the high road,' the one that leads you out of the present, physical world to the higher realms of spirit where your soul's thirst is quenched. Spirituality is the non-physical element that gives reason and meaning to your life.

Religion began as a human act of validating spiritual practice. For example, it is like when you have found a good thing, a spiritual truth, then all of a sudden someone tries to 'bottle it.' Religion was founded on spiritual principles but has been 'bought and sold' many times throughout your long history. It has gotten so very far off-course from its original intention that we now revisit the Earth to wake you from the deep sleep and to re-introduce these higher realms of spirit to you.

We walk beside you, joining spirit with matter once again. Awakening your spirituality is key on an individual level. We say it is fine to gather together with friends to celebrate your rituals and come together in prayer inside the walls of your churches, but we say unto you that true spirit is within the heart, in the higher realms of being. Go within those walls and unlock that door."

Q. What can I do to let God flow through me, to be connected with God, and to feel His Presence all the time?

"We say unto you, go within, listen and trust the guidance you receive from your heart. After some practice, you will have an inner knowing and this will no longer seem like an impossibility to you. Riding your first bike was difficult until you learned to balance yourself upon it. This is really the same thing.

We ask you to contemplate these questions... have you ever asked spirit to be with you? Have you ever given yourself permission to have the faith you desire?

We say unto you, give yourself the permission to have God's Presence within you and erase from your being all other notions that lead you astray from this. Then ask, believing you have already received, and allow the Universe to give unto you, and it is done.

Blessings abound, allow yourself permission to receive and think of nothing else than this."

A Meditation for Love and Light

"Breathe deeply, breathe very deeply. As you do this beautiful exercise, think only on this - that you breathe in the very substance of Light and Love itself. And as you breathe, visualize this Love-Light substance going inside your body, into all the darkened chambers, within all the organs... from your head, throat, back, spine, around to your heart, stomach, hands, arms, legs, feet... filling all the parts and spaces between the parts with Love/Light.

See your body fill with this radiant Light as though you are walking through a beautiful palace, flipping on the light switch in every room and passageway. See the brilliance of this Light and meditate on this. Direct this God-Light substance toward any wounds of yesterday. See the darkness vanishing into the Light and see yourself as free. Forgive those you feel harmed you and know that they simply brought you a beautiful lesson your soul needed you to learn. Bless the love-in-action. Amen."

Q. Can I have true love and marriage and still balance that with the desire to achieve spiritual understanding?

"We say, you are a multi-dimensional being and you are on the Earth to express that. You are designed to handle many aspects of yourself simultaneously. We are here to tell you that you can have it all so why would you wish to limit yourself? True Love is gold to you. This is what you're panning for on the Earth. For you, the quest is to combine these ideals and be in harmony with yourself and the Universe on all levels. This is the lesson your soul has chosen to learn in this lifetime. Do not be so hard on yourself. You have been much too strict, unrelenting, in your pursuit of perfection. We say it is more important to have fun while in school than to be so hard on yourself that joy is forever lost.

Make joyful expressions and experiences your new goal now. Ease up on yourself without losing the values that are very dear to you. Remember, whatever you send out to those in your world; whatever thoughts you hold in your mind; whatever words you speak all form the reality in which you walk.

Let go of the rules of your forefathers and choose to live your life in the now – completely in the moment you are in. When you arrive in the next moment, be in that moment completely, and so on. Restructure your living habit. Fear not that love is over with and not worth saving. Let that go and stay in the moment. Value what experience you have now and forget about what tomorrow might bring. You shall never enjoy your life until you have mastered focusing on this single moment and the joy it brings."

Q. Is there really a Great White Brotherhood of Light, and what purpose does it serve?

"Our Dear Fellow Spirits in Earth who are under the influence of separation, you are the only ones who could ask such a question! We say that you cannot, with the minds and bodies given you in Earth, see the Oneness of which you ask. But that's all right, you see, for if you were to know the totality of all things, you could not do the work that takes you there. This is all part of the Divine Plan.

God created you to have, what you term 'separate bodies' and separate personalities called 'mind,' but you are not separate in spirit. This was done to achieve one purpose, for God to express every aspect of Himself. It was never intended for you to forget your Divine Connection to Source, the One you call God, but after time rolled out its long days on Earth, your minds did, indeed, forget.

Now is the dawn of what is termed, 'The New Age of Light and Wisdom,' which is returning to your Earth now. Embrace this time with all your beingness, for it is time you remember your Oneness with all of life. This is what The Great White Light is all about. It has returned to Earth to bring you home to the Heaven you forgot about.

The Great White Brotherhood is the Oneness, it is the All, it is the One. You are an aspect of it, as are all others who are walking in human clothing. Be kind to one another in every action, thought, or step you take, for it is this kindness extended that reaches back to you. The circle complete, you return to Source, your home in Oneness with All That Is. The separation is real to you where you abide now, but shall not preside over what your Father has given you. Reach to Him with Love, and in his arms He shall lift you up and take you home."

217

Strength

"Man's mind, once stretched by a new idea, never regains its original dimension." -Oliver Wendell Holmes

Q. Life is so rushed that I find myself getting up in the morning running a race to see how much I can accomplish. I am too tired to do the things I want to do. Help!

"It is important that you gather yourself together and take a moment of rest and rejuvenation. Slowing down the fast pace will actually give you more time to do everything, and do it with joy, rather than from obligation. Breathe deeply and relax. Feel your connection with Mother Earth, regardless where you are, but try to be in nature if possible.

Garner your strength. Ask for guidance. Say words of renewal every morning and prayers of gratitude in the evening, and you shall be guided through whatever obstacle comes your way, and given God's Strength to deal with it in the way He would. Know that the road you travel has not been an easy one to navigate, but the power inherent in you is capable of accomplishing much more than you have imagined. Know that you are given the strength you need and release the worry you hold over this.

All that happens to you and in your world comes to you by rights of consciousness. What you have is yours by the law of 'like attracts like.' There is really nothing magical about this. Your life force or consciousness is always gaining in strength and this propensity urges you to reach higher than you have before.

What we see is that humans try to hold onto something that was, rather than practice a continual letting-go and welcoming the new into their life. This is where madness arises to create havoc within your hearts and minds. It is the basic need to trust in your divine nature to bring about the highest, best possible good to you, and to bring it to you continually throughout your lifetime and beyond.

Don't judge yourself too harshly for what has past, for who you were, or what you did before. Let the new energies arrive to renew you in body, mind and spirit. Stop getting yourself stuck in the muck of the past. It's over. All that remains is a blessing. We say, bless it, bless yourself for accomplishing it, and let it go. If you keep looking toward the past, you will miss new opportunities presenting themselves to you here and now.

We say, rely on the gift of inner strength that God has given you. It will always be there as your tool and ally, and is activated when you call upon it. Bring your power home to you. Do not let anyone take your power away from you, and they cannot do so unless you allow it to happen.

Here is a prayer for you to say until you feel strong and in control again..."

A Prayer For Inner Strength

"Thank you, God for granting me the courage to match the strength that sees me through my daily life. With your Light guiding me, I know my days are perfectly balanced with the love and strength to do all I have to do. I am healed, whole and perfectly renewed with every task that I must do.

I walk forward now, knowing I am blessed and knowing I am worthy to carry out what it is you would have me do. I am open to your voice and healing powers. Let my mind listen and my heart follow what it is you would have me do. I am new on this path, and ask that you show me a sign that I am on the highest possible path for a radiant life.

I Am the Light I Seek. I was made in God's perfect image. I am the Light I seek. My angels surround me with calm and sweet peace. I relax and breathe in this Love, and I am safe. God's strength is my safety now. Amen."

Taxes

*Q. How can I balance the need to pay property taxes
with the desire to be sovereign and free from government
tyranny?*

"Ah, a lesson all of mankind has faced, sworn to, sworn
at, rejected, honored and has murdered over. We say, give
unto Caesar what is Caesar's. This is an old, old truth you
humans have laid down as law so very long ago, but never
really figured another way, a better way of running government that would work better for you, so you begrudgingly
put up with old laws.

We see there are going to be some changes in the Earth
that are so great, so vast in nature, that it is impossible for
us to reveal all of it to you at this time, and for many reasons. One reason is that we intend not to instill any fear
about this, for it is human nature to fear any change at all,
even if it means good changes.

You must know in your heart, and always remember,
that your government is but a reflection of the society it represents. The arm of government moves very slowly – as
does creation – in the physical realms. Remember this and
save yourself a lot of grief and worry.

We see much discontent in the hearts of people with
how things are run by your government. It was never
intended to happen, but the ego has taken over its rule in
your third dimensional reality. Where love once ruled, fear
has taken its place. Until people in your society wake-up to
their hearts calling them home to the God self within them,
the ego will seemingly prevail.

But alas, there is hope. There are tremendous changes

coming into your Earth now. We say unto you, do not worry about anyone outside of yourself. Take care that you are acting from Love and keep extending that love in all you do, in every moment of every day. *Love is contagious!* People respond to love with love. Forget about watching what your neighbors are doing, or not doing, for this is how mankind got into the duality they seem to be in now.

Start with yourself. Speak from your own heart, act from Love in all your dealings in the world you find yourself in, and in your releasing your ego-creations, you are released. Remove the painful circumstances out of the context in which you are viewing them and place them in the Light of pure Consciousness and Love. Trust that what occurs has happened as a gift to you. Answer that inner call to awaken and be in the day you are in today. Stop living your life in the future.

Everyone on Earth has their own agenda and lessons to deal with and we suggest that you bless them by sending Love and Light to them without further judgment. Hatred never healed a thing. Love heals it all.

Let this Love-Light wash over you like a shower direct from the heavens. This is your lesson in forgiveness and in letting go. You see, it is in letting go what you think is real, that you gain what is eternal. Forgive your government for they are just a manifestation of the present consciousness of the people. In your mind, let God (good) prevail, letting it guide your ways and all your affairs. When you change, the world seemingly changes to accommodate your shift in consciousness.

When paying your taxes, we say bless the money as it goes and does its good work through the people who will be receiving it. Never forget that it shall once again return to you ten times greater. We see that when one sends out anger and bitterness when paying their share, more bitterness and more anger return.

Your job now is to release your anger and know that what you send out comes back. Turn that anger into gratitude and see your life literally do an about face. Make a list of all the things you are grateful for instead of rehashing the list of injustices and grievances. You will see your life change.

We promise you that what you complain about today shall disappear in the love you abide in tomorrow just by refocusing on what it is you truly want in your life and releasing that which you don't. Be watchful over your thoughts as you are changing this paradigm within you. Whatever is in your thinking (mind) and feeling (heart) shall reproduce itself in your life ten times over.

We see that money is just another "prop" in the play called life. It is just energy that takes on whatever emotion you give it. Therefore, we suggest that you always bless it as it passes through your hands and goes into another's hands. See your cash traveling the globe doing good works wherever it goes. Then see it traveling once again, returning to you to be blessed and sent out again. You will then experience the truest riches of Earth.

We bless you on your newfound journey exploring the many wonderful dimensions of your heart. Your life shall be truly blessed as you choose to go forth on this path."

Trust

"Trust would solve every problem now." - A Course In Miracles

Q. How can I stop worrying and start trusting?

"We say unto you, Dear Ones, in the very same way you have always trusted Mother Nature to produce the green grass and blue sky; the sun to rise every morning and to set at night, we say you need to allow and trust life to flow through you now. Trust that your purpose unfolds according to a greater plan set in motion by Divine Intelligence. The power that is in Mother Nature is also in you and in the situation that is concerning you. You do not need to direct the show telling Her what to do and when to do it. All you need do is *trust.*

Let go and let the 'would-be-stress' travel through you unencumbered and back into nothingness from whence it came. Reroute this creative juice into something you desire to accomplish and put this energy to work *for* you rather than *against* you. Rather than your old way of worrying what will happen and be fearful that only tragedy and darkness looms around you, allow wonder to fill you up instead.

Change your thought pattern and say, "I wonder how God will handle this situation?"

And by all means, get excited about it! Anticipating miracles is what sets the stage for miracles! Thought begets thought and the 'creative juice' is neutral. It matters not if you wonder about things or worry about things. We say unto you, choose which you prefer. Change worry into wonder. It is that simple. This allows God to be present in your life and for a miracle to occur."

Unworthiness

"Your task is not to seek for love, but merely to seek and find all of the barriers within yourself that you have built against it.

- A Course In Miracles

Q. My feelings of unworthiness hold me in darkness and keep me sad. I know this is not God's Will for me, but how can I reverse these feelings?

"We say to you, the only purpose darkness holds is for you to know what Light is, for without darkness, there is nothing to measure Light. You didn't know you were perfect and lived in perfect divine oneness with God, in Heaven (Light) until you created the opposite – Earth (dark). But in this mis-creating, you kept elements of Heaven alive in your heart, the center of your universe, and have called these angels.

The angels are present whenever you have true joy in your heart. By joy we do not mean happiness, for happiness is simply a reaction to what someone else has done to affect you and make you happy. Joy is born within your own internal heart and springs forth like a fountain, without pause and without end. Think of what brings you joy and what has brought you happiness.

We say you will know the difference in your own comparisons. It is joy you are now seeking in your life and not happiness. Your heart has opened and is poised to experience True Love and True Joy and it will not settle for less than that ever again. Your heart wants more than it has had before, and we say that this is the mission you are on.

We say, forgive yourself. Believe you are worthy of God's Light and Love. You live in it! We say that this will restore your worthiness. Let the old days be gone. You need never punish yourself again. All you really need do is love and release these thoughts of punishment and you are free. The aches you feel are but reminders of the lifetime you sought to punish yourself in the name of God. God never ordered punishment on man. Man created his own guilt and the punishment that would alleviate it.

Now, release this need in you that says you are guilty and unworthy, for you have come into this lifetime to complete this erroneous belief. Decide to forgive your belief in unworthiness and release it from you now. Repeat the following meditation until your heart accepts your new message that you are, indeed, Truth, Love and Beauty and nothing else. Walk in the Light and Love of God *and know that you do.*"

A Prayer To Release Unworthiness

"I love and approve of myself. I am a loving, talented child of the Creator. I am an important part of the Divine Plan and I accept this Plan for me now. I am guided and directed in such ways that allow my unfoldment and my learning to take place. I am always safe in the present moment, for I know in my heart I am where I am for good reason and Divine purpose. I choose to walk in God's Light today.

My feet are sure of every step as they take me where I need to be for my true fulfillment now and always. My body reflects to the outer world my peace within. I am safe and happy in this and every moment knowing that my highest good awaits my unfoldment to it. I am on my right path. I am safe and I am deeply loved. So be it. Amen."

Weariness

"You don't drown by falling in the water;
you drown by staying there." -Edwin Louis Cole

Q. Sreper, why is it that so many souls in Earth are feeling weary?

"Dear Ones, you have been walking endlessly in your illusions of illusions. You've gotten so deeply enmeshed in the quagmire of your little world that you have lost sight of the real world. In some cases, we see that you have lost yourselves. This has tired you out!

Your angels and guides in the unseen and sacred worlds are calling you home and out of your dreams now. We see vast confusion spreading out upon your planet, but we say that this is temporary until you decide to wake up, turn-off the alarm clock and walk with us into the Light of this New Day in the new world.

We have come for you! The prophecies are fulfilled!

This is what many call 'the Second Coming of the Dawn of Light on Earth' and the birth of Light within the heart of each and everyone of you. We, the messengers of Light, come to you through many channels, through every soul. Be certain that our message will not be missed, or misunderstood this time.

The weariness you have been feeling has been caused by your looking outward for the Divine connection while it has been within you always. Seek and find it there. Looking outwardly will only tire you out.

All who cry with desire to return home shall return home. Some will hear this calling in a song, some will hear the words from a friend, some will read our words in this book! Some will awaken on their own, their hearts resonating with the higher frequencies that have been prompting them, and some will learn to hear *their inner voice* speaking to them. These are all good channels. They all carry the same message and direct you to awaken, to remember who you really are, to put that message in your heart and to take that knowledge home.

The time is now. The Plan unfolds. As the words of Jesus said, 'Come onto me all who are weary and heavy laden and I will give you rest.'"

Weather and other
Thought Patterns

"Experience is often what you get when you were
expecting something else." - Unknown

Q. Sreper, why is the weather so out of sorts? It often feels as though the whole world has turned upside-down because the weather is so unusual. People are snow skiing in June! Is El Niño over or will it continue to torment us? If this is a symptom of the need for our planet to heal, how can we help?

"We begin by saying that the weather patterns are a direct reflection of internal, or emotional weather patterns held within human consciousness. If you, as a people, are in a state of emotional upheaval, you will create upheaval in your weather patterns. If you find yourself in a peaceful frame of mind, your weather shall also be peaceful and calm. The more frantic people become if they focus on the ills of the world, storms are created.

The weather isn't thrust upon you as a means of punishment. Like everything else on the Earth plane, the weather is created by your prevailing thought patterns. You create the weather but you've been on Earth for so long that you've forgotten the power you wield. In this, and in most other things you experience on that plane, weather patterns are a reflection of what mass-consciousness is expecting. Weather patterns are asking you to wake up and pay attention. Call your power home. See how powerful you really are. Begin now to focus on what you want to create and stop wasting your energy.

The roar of Earth's loudspeakers (the news media) had ought to be quieted so everyone could once again become still and focused on their own life and not worry over the ills of the rest of the world. You are given way too much to be concerned with, thanks to your news media. It was never meant for you to carry the weight of the world on your shoulders. Yet, when you turn on your TV sets and radios, you get blasted with every detail in the world.

These stories are brought to you as though you alone can solve the world's problems! We say stand back. Take a stand and turn within yourselves to the peaceful state that once was there. Dig deep, for inner peace is buried.

El Nino, first of all, is a direct creation of excess pent-up frustration within the collective consciousness. The energy has to go somewhere. Human consciousness has all but lost contact with their spirit and why they are on the planet in the first place, which is to give and receive love.

When you see violent storms hit hard, we say this is not some sort of punishment from a cruel and unforgiving God, for this is a myth you bought into and believed. We say the answer to calming the storms is within you. Become still and peaceful. Then, you radiate peace outwardly and you create a peaceful world where you are centered on yourself and your goals of harmony and love.

If you stay focused on the outer world and what is happening next in your weather, we say you become unnerved and anxious, and all you will see is chaos, disorder and stormy weather. The choice is yours to make. Call back your power to yourself and meditate on the weather you would rather experience.

We say that if you do this and your next door neighbor does not, when any 'Earth changes' come your way, you will be left standing while his house and life is washed away. This choice is yours to make by choosing on what you would create as your reality."

Q. Will these patterns continue?

"Let us answer you by asking you a question. Will your belief system that supports them continue? You decide!

Create only the good, the beautiful and the holy! Be a Lightworker – one who knows the truth and brings the Light in for others until they awaken and can find their way. You are there to face fear and then heal it. You are there to give and receive love. That is the only real reason you're on Earth.

Remember, too, that everything has consciousness. You communicate with everything through your thoughts which resonate and carry a vibration that attracts like vibrations to you. Give love and you receive love. Give fear and you receive fear. You communicate your thoughts to other people, to your pets and to the weather! They all reflect back to you whatever emotion you send out – love begets love; hate begets hate; impatience begets impatience, etc.

We say this is why when you see a dog, for example, the dog immediately knows if you like him or if you are afraid of him. Watch this next time you see an animal. Notice what thought you are sending out to the animal and check the response. Listen to your pets and ask them what they are in your life to teach you. Ask them what your connection to them is. What is the reason you are together at this time?

Listen for their answer which will come intuitively. This may take a little while and a little practice for the animals have fallen silent in their communication with humans due to the long sleep you have been under.

Now, we also say this is similar in your weather patterns, too. A weather pattern is simply a thought. Change the thought and see what happens. Always, always ask for permission from the universe first before delving into changing such patterns. Stop the mischievous behavior you are known for, and be responsible for your creations. You will be shocked at the personal power you truly have if you but started to take notice of it.

Awaken, Dear Ones, and do it gently – under Divine Law so as not to hurt yourselves or anyone else."

Willingness

"Personally, I'm always ready to learn, although I do not always like being taught." -Winston Churchill

Q. Sreper, how can I let go of my defenses? Even though I realize my defenselessness stands in the way of my good, I am not always willing to be willing. Help!

"Dear Ones, your life in Earth school could be so much easier on you if you but ask for one thing... to have a willing heart. This takes desire, and we say desire emerges from your soul's experience of Earth living. It takes contemplation to see there is another Avenue of Light that you could be on. And it takes practice.

Ask your angels to bless you with the willingness it takes for your human eyes to see and your heart to feel.

Know that very few things are being withheld from humanity anymore. There are no great secrets cloaked in the darkness of the ages past. You will see the ancient mysteries coming to life in your everyday life.

This is a thrilling time to be present on the planet and we hope that this will encourage you to become open and willing to receive your greater good. It doesn't take genius minds or years in solitary meditative practices upon a mountaintop to become enlightened. That was the truth then, this is now.

Ask to be willing and let the angels of God do the rest! Let go all your old ideas. This is a brand new paradigm you are experiencing on Earth now. We are keeping your feet steady through the bumpy ride.

Things that once appeared to take a long time to develop – such as the quality of willingness, now takes only the desire and the openness to receive it.

Simply clear the debris away and let willingness reign.

You need do nothing more than receive all the good that comes rushing in. After that, you will not consider holding the state of unwillingness again.

A Prayer For Willingness

"Dear God, I ask to be willing to step up to the Light... to be who I am meant to be – an extension of you – and experience life as I have never before experienced life. God grant me the willingness to be a luminary of Your Divine Will.

Place in me your spark – your Divine essence that is my inheritance, and align my will with yours. Open my heart to the willingness I need to stop limiting myself and to accept my good now. Use me, Dear God, as your shining example. Let me be an inspiration in the world of hearts that I touch, and leave in my wake a legacy of Light for those who follow in my footsteps.

Let your glow be my glow. Let your radiance be my radiance. Let it wash over me permeating every cell until I am filled with your dazzling peace. Should I resist, give me the steps to become willing and open. Guide me to see that your way is greater than mine, and the rewards much greater. Amen."

"So, Dear Ones, put your dancing shoes on. The glorious dance is about to begin!"

Pass the Torch
Closing Words from Sreper

"Remember that fear is what you have been creating
and not what Heaven would give you." -Sreper

"May Heaven help you on your journey toward the Light of Life, and we say that more Light is available to you now than ever before. Along with your desire for wisdom and understanding, a flood of Light shall pour over you and bless your life. Where there has been a shadow, fear not, for there is a spark igniting the dawn of this glorious new age.

Now, Dear Ones, as we close this book, we pass the torch. We say unto you who are the Lightbearers, you have been steadfast in God's Divine Mission to carry forth His work, the work of the unseen realms in Earth, and now your reward of peace shall prevail. It shall come upon you as never before.

We ask that you bask in the Light of this new day for it is your inheritance from your grateful Father. Know in your hearts that God and His angels bless you – each and every-one – and watch over you as you journey forth into your life. Carry God's Love in your heart and His message to your fellow travelers, as we do, and together we shall Light the world, the likes of which it has never seen. Go in peace, Dear Ones, go in peace."

Epilogue

Looking back over the last twelve years and considering the hundreds of messages I received from the angels, I find there is a notable golden thread that weaves itself through them all. Some may think the messages are redundant, but there is a good reason for that. It is the same ancient lesson of love and forgiveness repeating itself. It is the same lesson we all must learn, and the angels are making sure that we will finally get it. It is the miracle that changes life.

Over and over again we will hear these words. We have heard them hundreds of times already. It is the bottom line of any spiritual path, and the final line of this book. Regardless of what our problem is, and no matter how it has manifested in our lives, we must ask, "Am I willing to forgive?"

The Gold we seek is in becoming truly ready to love ourselves as God does, and offer that love to others. And, if we are not ready to do this, there is no judgment, but the message will repeat itself in a variety of ways, perhaps, until we finally hear it. Let us pray.

Prayer to Light My Way

"Dear God, Light the way. Let me be willing to do only Your Will for me now and from this day forward. This doesn't mean sacrificing my will, but aligning it with my heart's higher purpose, which holds the same goal as Yours.

And, Dear Father, may Your sweet peace prevail, and let not our hearts and minds want for anything less than what You would have for us. Amen."

About the Author

Rev. Nancy Freier is an intuitive spiritual counselor with a fascinating life story who has been a featured guest on many radio and television programs. She has received an honorary Ph.D. in Counseling for her more than 12 years of work in this field. An ordained minister in the Order of Melchizedek, Nancy channels the angels. She is also flower essence practitioner, an interior designer and a Certified Feng Shui consultant. Rev. Freier is a survivor of two near-death experiences and with help from the angels, she overcame an 18-year addiction to alcohol (1984) and cigarettes (1993). She began to consciously hear the angels on the day her fiancé died, November 18, 1986.

Fulfilling her promise to make help available to others who suffered, she began writing a column called *Angel Talk* to share their wisdom. *Angel Talk* now appears in a growing list of publications. Its popularity led her to publishing *The Inner Voice* magazine, in print from 1991 to 1998, it was converted to an online magazine in 1997 and has become an internationally popular website.

Spiritual counseling with the angels is available to everyone through her *Spiritual First-Aid* message board and *Ask An Angel for a Prayer* ministry. Private readings and Feng Shui consultations are also available. A big part of Nancy's ministry is to teach people how to communicate with their angels and guides in spirit in a class called *You Can Talk To Your Angels* based on her book by the same name. She and her partner, Jim Clark travel and teach this empowering workshop. Nancy is employed as a copy editor for *The Desert Sun* newspaper in Palm Springs, California.

For more information, please contact:
Lightlines Publishing Company;
P.O. Box 2838; Palm Desert, CA 92261-2838;
Phone: (760)568-9802;
E-mail: nancy@theinnervoice.com

Lightlines Publishing Order Form

(Please check items requested and indicate quantity ordered)

❏ Qty____**HEAVEN HELP ME! A CELESTIAL GUIDE TO HEALING** • $12.95; Book by Nancy Freier. ISBN: 1-930126-02-6

❏ Qty____**HEAVEN HELP ME! A CELESTIAL GUIDE TO HEALING** • $10; An audio tape version of selected prayers from the angels, read by the author. ISBN: 1-930126-03-4

❏ Qty____**YOU CAN TALK TO YOUR ANGELS** • $12
A workbook by Nancy Freier, it is the study guide used by students in the class by the same name. ISBN: 1-930126-04-2

❏ Qty____**YOU CAN TALK TO YOUR ANGELS** • $10
Audio tape with "Meet Your Angels" by Nancy Freier and Jim Clark; and "The Great White Light Healing Meditation" by Nancy Freier. Music by Richard Jerome Bennett. ISBN: 1-930126-05-0

❏ Qty____ **THE INNER VOICE MAGAZINE**
Timeless, inspirational reading! 1 set of 12 back issues for $10

Amount of order: $_____
Add shipping (see note below $_____
Total $_____

PLEASE NOTE: Add $2 per item to cover postage and handling costs to US addresses. Add $6 (in US funds) for foreign shipments.
Credit card users: Order any of these items online from our website!

Your Name _____

Street _____

City/State/Zip _____

Phone _____

E-mail: _____

Lightlines Publishing Company
P.O. Box 2838
Palm Desert, CA 92261-2838
Phone/fax: (760) 568-9802
E-mail: lightlines@theinnervoice.com
Website: www.theinnervoice.com
Thank you!

239